TEACHING SCIENCE
TO CHILDREN

GARLAND REFERENCE LIBRARY
OF SOCIAL SCIENCE
(VOL. 304)

TEACHING SCIENCE
TO CHILDREN
A Resourcebook

Mary D. Iatridis

with a chapter by
Phylis Morrison

GARLAND PUBLISHING, INC. · NEW YORK & LONDON
1986

Library of Congress Cataloging-in-Publication Data

Iatridis, Mary D., 1928–
Teaching science to children.

(Garland reference library of social science ;
v. 304)
Includes indexes.
1. Science—Study and teaching—Bibliography.
2. Science—Juvenile literature—Bibliography.
3. Handicapped children—Education—Science—
Bibliography.   I. Title.   II. Series.
Z5818.S3I25   1986   [LB1532]   016.3723′5044   84-48879
ISBN 0-8240-8747-X (alk. paper)

Printed on acid-free, 250-year-life paper
Manufactured in the United States of America

CONTENTS

PREFACE

This book is a labor of love for children and
science and it is based on the assumption that science
learning for children is as essential as reading,
writing, and arithmetic. The books I reviewed reflect
a commitment to this premise and although authors may
disagree on approaches, strategies, and content, they
all state strong and convincing arguments on the contributions of science teaching to the intellectual
development of children.

The golden era of science curriculum from the
1960s echoes throughout the bibliography with the
prevailing view that science be taught as a combination of process and content.

The book is written for educators of young children
(teachers in traditional and non-traditional settings)
with the idea that through the multiplicity of approaches on how to teach science presented in the book,
they may search and identify the one most suitable to
them.

It has been a challenge to track down books on
how to teach science (Part I) and books with science
activities that will engage children in learning science (Part II). At times it was hard to decide in
which category to place certain books because of the
intermingling of methodology and activities in their
content. I hope my decision will not discourage the
reader from using the books.

Finally, Part III lists and reviews science books
for children, a contribution of Phylis Morrison, an
educator and book critic of long standing, specifically,

on children's books in science. This part includes a
selective bibliography of different types of books in
science that are available. It will be of special
interest to teachers and will encourage them to integrate reading with their curriculums of science.

Teaching Science to Children

Chapter 1

TEXTBOOKS

Introduction

Science teaching for children has been greatly
influenced during the past twenty-five years both by
the educational world and by scientific knowledge.
More specifically, contributions to the field have
been made from the following areas: child development
and learning theories, curriculum organization and
development, materials and content, social attitudes
and values, and evaluation systems. Textbooks on the
subject reflect a wide variety of approaches ranging
from the teacher-centered view that the accumulation
of factual scientific knowledge is the desirable outcome of children's learning to the child-centered discovery approach where the process and the children's
experience themselves are the focus.

Child Development and Learning Theories

Essential to all books published on teaching
science to children is the author's viewpoint on how
children develop intellectually and how they learn
effectively. The theories that prevail in most
writings reflect those developed by Piaget, Bruner,

and Gagné. Certain authors base the teaching of science on one theory more than another while others rely on an eclectic model that incorporates each theory selectively.

Piaget's developmental theory explains how children learn in a sequence of stages and how each stage utilizes and assimilates the preceding stage. The four major stages are: sensory-motor (0-3 years), preoperational (3-6 years), concrete operations (6-11 years), and formal operations (11 years to adult). The child's many experiences during each stage contribute greatly to his development. Piaget claims that children must experience the physical world so that they may gain knowledge of it.

Children experience objects and physical phenomena and understand them according to their current developmental level. For example, children in the preoperational stage explain the phenomena around them perceptually--"how they look"--and not logically-- "how they really are"--which will be the understanding in later stages. We know that children at the early stage lack the ability to coordinate variables and cannot view the idea of an object having several properties; the concept of conservation has not developed yet and the child cannot reverse thought.[1]

The author's view on child development has a serious impact on the organization of science curriculum and the teaching strategies that are used. From a Piagetian perspective children's interactions with the physical world are important because it is through such experiences that they understand and learn about the properties of materials and phenomena. For example, materials sink or float as the child works with them in a water environment; young children will predict that large things will sink while older students may have different comments.

If Piaget focused on children's developmental stages, Jerome Bruner examined "the act of learning." His widely quoted hypothesis "any subject can be taught effectively in some intellectually honest form to any child at any stage of development" has greatly influenced the structure and organization of science curricula in schools. The learning process according to Bruner is a three-stage sequence: (1) the individual's information acquisition, (2) the transformation or manipulation of this information by the individual in determining whether it serves adequately the new tasks,[2] and (3) "the learning episode" is accommodated, depending on the capabilities of the learner. This theory accommodates children at different developmental stages and suggests a spiral sequence of curriculum so that the act of learning for the same content can be reenacted several times through the course of the child's life. For example, magnets can be taught several times because the "act of learning" for the child will be a new learning experience each time.

Another theorist who examined the act of learning in a more systematic way is Robert Gagné. He considered the process of scientific research and adapted it to the teaching of science to children and concluded that scientific inquiry is the most desirable learning process for students to follow when they study science.[3] Furthermore, he claimed that scientific inquiry as a process for learning science can be applied to younger students, provided the conditions of instruction employed comply with the goals appropriate for that age group.

Scientific inquiry proceeds in a stage-like manner. This systematic, problem-solving, thinking process can begin with children at the kindergarten level where they begin to acquire competencies that contribute to the process of scientific inquiry. The competencies the learner must acquire to proceed with the inquiry method are: observing, figuring, measuring, orienting things in space, describing and classifying objects and events, inferring and making conceptual models.[4] Such competencies are only the beginning of learning and do not confine their usefulness to science alone but to any body of knowledge where inquiry can be applied.

Criteria in
Organization and Development

In the organization and development of science curriculum, there are two prevailing approaches: the inquiry process that Gagné promoted and the child-centered approach that builds on Piagetian development theory.

The science curriculum based on Gagné arranges subject matter or content in a hierarchical fashion. Gagné provides evidence that learning materials can be planned and sequenced in a way similar to the scientific process. This learning model has been the basis for a science curriculum like S-APA (Science A Process Approach) developed by the National Science Foundation in the mid 1960s.[5]

The child-centered emphasis focuses on children's developmental levels, takes into account children's views about the physical world and builds on them. Although inquiry is incorporated in child-centered curricula, the emphasis remains on the way the children explore the materials and how they integrate them into their lives. The ESS (Elementary Science Study) is an example of a child-centered science curriculum that was also developed by the National Science Foundation in the mid 1960s.[6]

The books reviewed generally reflect one of these two approaches. Other works cited employ a combination of the two.

Content and Materials

It is widely accepted that interactions with materials are essential in the teaching of science so children can learn about the properties of objects as well as other physical phenomena. During the 1960s the National Science Foundation (N.S.F.) funded four major science curriculum programs for children in grades K through 8: COPES (Conceptually Oriented Pro-

gram in Elementary Science), ESS (Elementary Science
Study), S-APA (Science A Process Approach), and SCIS
(Science Curriculum Improvement Study). These programs relate closely to prevailing theories of learning. The content and materials for all programs aim
to enhance children's conceptual thinking and understanding of science by using the process of scientific
inquiry.

The literature in early childhood education supports the idea that varied science experiences for
young children are effective ways for learning science
especially when they relate to the environment the
children are familiar with. The quality of the experience the child has depends on the materials and
how they are presented to him. It is important for
young children to engage in sensory explorations because their sensory systems are their investigating
tools. Therefore, sensory observations and perceptual
discrimination assist in the sorting of objects and
phenomena that are desirable outcomes of the inquiry
process.[7,8]

"What kind of science?" becomes more of an issue
during the elementary grades. The diverse viewpoints
on what science to teach are wide and are reflected
in science sourcebooks and in the four programs
created by the N.S.F.

Social Attitudes and Values

One of the reasons why the quality and the content
of science teaching varies from school to school can
be directly attributed to the societal forces that
influence curriculum in schools. The local management
of the education process is responsible for the type
of science programs that prevail in a school. As a
result, in recent times, environmental concerns have
increased the teaching of ecology, pollution, nutrition and nuclear fallout. In her book, *Teaching
Science as a Continuous Inquiry*, Mary B. Rowe alerts
educators to the fact that "science is the central

enterprise of the societies populating the planet earth during the 20th century" and cautions educators to "find out how science is affecting us and what we can do about it."[9] It appears that for some educators the social implications are the focus of science teaching while others look at scientific literacy and education as a key to national supremacy in the technological race.

Regardless of orientation, societal forces control budgetary sources and as a result have a direct effect on "what science" should be taught to children. It should be noted that not all the books on how to teach science indicate concerns about value implications in science curriculum.

Evaluation Systems

The implementation of a science curriculum is closely related to its method of evaluation. Evaluation techniques are widely discussed in most textbooks and are as diverse as the answers to "why science for children?" Guidelines for evaluation come from various sources. Some curriculum developers follow Bloom's taxonomy in setting objectives and devising instruments to measure the effectiveness of achieving these objectives. Other educators consider the overt behavior of the children as the source of evaluation. However, the problems of reliability and validity in such observational methodology hinder the promotion of science programs that favor the interactive process as the focal point of teaching science. No doubt, pressure for accountability favors science programs that provide measuring devices like tests while other programs with more appeal to teachers and children have been curtailed because there has been a lack of credible evaluative data.

In summary, the books that have emerged as textbooks in the teaching of science to children during the past twenty-five years reflect a gamut of teaching methodologies. For example, a book such as

E. Victor's classic *Science for the Elementary School* represents an eclectic model in the teaching of science. It informs teachers of the theories explaining children's learning and their implications for teaching strategies. The guidelines indicate how the "process of science" has become more than the "content." The emphasis on the "process of science" as a basis for curriculum organization and teaching strategy prevails in most books that qualify as textbooks on teaching science to children. The differences among these books can be found in the organization and implementation of the inquiry process and in the content recommended for teaching.

"Scientific and social inquiry go hand in hand in the world we now face" claims Mary B. Rowe.[10] She emphasizes the need for integrating science in our everyday teaching because of the effect science has on our everyday living. Furthermore, she recommends that children must be taught the scientific process in relation to issues that affect daily life such as pollution, nutrition and ecology.

Child-centered considerations in teaching science prevail in Doris C. Trojcak's book, *Science with Children*.[11] She states that affective and cognitive goals must intermingle. The attitudes of teachers towards science must also be dealt with and their fears resolved so that science will have an appeal to them and they in turn will facilitate children's science learning.

This is only a sample of the range of content and viewpoints that appear in the many existing books in science teaching.

NOTES

1. Chittenden, Ed A. "Piaget in Elementary Science Education." *Science and Children*. 8, No. 4 (Dec. 1970), 9-15.

2. Bruner, Jerome. *The Process of Education.* Cambridge, Mass.: Harvard University Press, 1960.

3. Gagné, R. "The Learning Requirements for En-
quiry." *Journal of Research in Science Teaching.*
1, Issue 2 (1963), 144-153.

4. Ibid.

5. Waters, Barbara S. *Science Can Be Elementary.*
New York: Citation Press, 1973.

6. Ibid.

7. Lansdown, Brenda, et al. *Teaching Elementary
Science.* New York: Harcourt Brace Jovanovich, 1971.

8. Elkind, David. "Piaget and Science Education."
Science and Children. 10, No. 3 (Nov. 1972), 9-12.

9. Rowe, Mary B. *Teaching Science as a Continuous
Inquiry: A Basic.* 2nd ed. New York: McGraw-Hill,
1978.

10. Ibid.

11. Trojcak, Doris C. *Science with Children.* New
York: McGraw-Hill, 1979.

BIBLIOGRAPHY

Abruscato, Joseph. *Teaching Children Science.* Engle-
    wood, Cliffs, N.J.: Prentice-Hall, 1982.

    The book is organized in three parts. Part I
analyzes theories of how children learn science,
discusses teaching and curriculum models, expands
on assessment techniques, and suggests ways to adapt
the teaching of science for handicapped and gifted
children. Parts II and III focus on science content
activities and methods. Earth, space, atmosphere,
weather, the cosmos, life sciences, and physical
science are fully developed topics. The chapters
on ecology and energy are particularly interesting.
The appendices include Piagetian tasks, the metric

system, and references to suppliers of science
materials and books on science teaching. The book
has a lively style and offers practical suggestions
for effective science teaching. The wide range of
topics can be appropriate for grades K-6 and will
interest teachers who want to venture seriously into
science teaching.

Almy, Millie. *Logical Thinking in the Second Grade*.
New York: Teachers' College Press, 1970.

The contribution of Almy to science education is
extensive. She researched "how children think,"
utilizing science materials and phenomena and Piagetian developmental theory. A most valuable book
for the science educator who wants documentation
through research.

Anastasiou, Clifford J. *Teachers, Children and
Things: Materials-Centered Science*. Minneapolis,
Minn.: Holt, Rinehart and Winston of Canada, 1971.

This book is concerned with the interaction between children and materials during the scientific
process. It describes activities for children and
offers tips to teachers on how to help them get involved. The author bases his teaching theories on
children's developmental stages and draws from the
psychological constructs of Piaget's developmental
theory and Torraine's work on creativity. A teacher
can facilitate inquiry and discovery through
materials found inside and outside the classroom. A
flow chart on school grounds from the Nuffield
teachers Guide on page 82 emphasizes further the
openness of this book. Its informal style is most
valuable for the teacher of young children who has
been apprehensive about teaching science.

Anderson, Ronald. *Developing Children's Thinking
Through Science*. Englewood Cliffs, N.J.: Prentice-
Hall, 1970.

This book takes a systematic approach to the relationship between science teaching and children's
thinking. It examines a sequence of philosophical
constructs on the question of what is science. The
book questions the belief that behavioral objectives
are the only approach to effective science teaching
and expands on the characteristics of problem-
solving and creativity in this field.

The author acknowledges the importance of developmental stages (Piaget) and the hierarchy of learning
(Gagné) and urges teachers to consider them in planning
science teaching. In curriculum design and resources,
Anderson offers a wide range of theoretical and
practical alternatives. He addresses teachers'
"areas of vital concern" during the teaching of
science and concludes with a wide range of evaluation guidelines. The book offers a very thorough
examination of all the issues that relate to the
teaching of science to children. It will be useful
to concerned teachers who want to go beyond lesson
plans and understand how children learn science and
who further wish to be effective as teachers of
science.

Blough, G.O., and Julius Schwartz. *Elementary School
Science and How to Teach It*. 7th ed. New York:
Holt, Rinehart and Winston, 1979.

This book, addressed to teachers of elementary
grades who teach science, is comprehensive and includes vast amounts of scientific information.
The first part is relatively brief (100 pages) and
offers an overview of what elementary science is
and how it can be taught. Techniques, strategies,
and resources are discussed and recommended. The
remainder of the book (approximately 500 pages)
offers science content classified into the areas of
earth, universe, living things, matter, and energy.
Each topic is discussed in terms of content and
teaching strategies.

Butts, David P. *Teaching Science in the Elementary School*. New York: The Free Press, 1975.

This book is more concerned with involving children in learning science than with the traditional over-views of goals, strategies, techniques, and re-sources that usually appear in science teaching books. In Part I the author states his philosophy and objectives, creating the framework for guiding and assessing the children's learning. Part II contains powerful ideas on how to involve children in learning through activities derived from the well-known science curricula of SCIS, S-APA and ESS. A science teacher will find this section most valu-able. Butts expresses his viewpoints through many anecdotal situations and assists teachers in devel-oping views, values, and judgments on teaching sci-ence to children.

Butts, David P., ed. *Research and Curriculum Develop-ment in Science Education*. Austin, Tex.: University of Texas Press, 1970.

An in-depth monograph on research in the teaching and learning of science. The research components focus on the educational experience and its conse-quences for learning. A significant contribution for scholars in science education who want to fur-ther their own research in the field of evaluation of science teaching.

Butts, David P., and Gene E. Hall. *Children and Science: The Process of Teaching and Learning*. Englewood Cliffs, N.J.: Prentice-Hall, 1975.

Organized in an innovative, self-directed manner, the book aims to instruct through activities that enable the reader to experience and understand the skills necessary for effective science learning. Some of the activities are selected from the well-known N.S.F. science education programs--ESS, SCIS, S-APA, Minnimast and others--and demonstrate the

diversity of approach and philosophy in the programs.
The chapters are titled informally: "Science is...,"
"Using Your Senses," "Telling Another Person,"
"Finding Out How Much More," "Communicating Change,"
"Explaining What You Observe," "Concluding an Ex-
periment," "Causes and Effects," "Defining Terms,"
"Searching for Patterns," "Generalizing," and
"Scientist at Work." The writing style has a sense
of immediacy that is reinforced by the conversational
tone of the author. The book is enjoyable and help-
ful especially for the teacher who may feel over-
whelmed at the idea of teaching science to children.

Cain, Sandra E., and Gail M. Evans. *Sciencing: An
Involvement Approach to Elementary Science Methods.*
2nd ed. Columbus, Ohio: Merrill, 1984.

Process skills are a feature of this book. The
authors introduce each chapter with a flowchart so
that the reader is guided through its content.
Chapter One summarizes the nature of science, children, and learning, and shows how an understanding
of this material contributes to the planning and
implementation of science teaching. Next follows
a discussion of the place of the laboratory approach,
textbooks, and text kits in science curricula. The
NSF programs on the '60s (S-APA, SCIS and ESS) are
reviewed as the classical laboratory approach curricula, and sample activities are presented from
each of them. The strengths and weaknesses of all
types of curricula are evaluated on the basis of
well-stated criteria. Text kits are singled out as
an acceptable alternative to science teaching.
Teachers' lesson planning and classroom management
are addressed and guidelines on teaching science
for the handicapped are developed. The potential
of microcomputers in science teaching receives
special recognition.

Finally, the book offers a wide variety of appendices. The most impressive is the review of the NSF
Elementary Science Programs. They are presented
historically, philosophically, and conceptually in

a content sequence. The book includes everything
you ever wanted to know about science and how to
teach it to children. However, it requires a
skilled reader of curricula body to utilize and appreciate its content. Its multiple charts and illustrations are exceptional.

Carin, Arthur A., and Robert B. Sund. *Teaching
Science Through Discovery*. 4th ed. Columbus,
Ohio: Merrill, 1980.

The authors suggest that the text be used as a
reference book on teaching science through discovery and indeed the book fulfills such criteria.
The first fifteen chapters emphasize strategies and
conditions for developing effective discovery lessons in science. Included are chapters on developing
questioning and sensitive listening techniques and
on creating and teaching discovery laboratory lessons. There is a survey of existing science programs
that incorporate discovery strategies and plans for
arranging classrooms to enhance individualized as
well as group teaching. Children's developmental
stages are considered and referred to throughout
the book and special effort is made to address
issues that relate to teaching science to preschoolers. Attention is given to integrating discovery science teaching with other subjects, and
evaluating the discovery method. Each chapter concludes with examples that contribute to concept
clarification. Illustrations and charts are helpful
and attractive.

The remainder of the book covers the content areas
of science--living, environmental, and physical.
The format follows an investigative and discovery
sequence that is most helpful to the teacher.

A special section is devoted to discovery activities for preschoolers. Piagetian tasks are presented
as reference points for children's levels of understanding. One of the appendices offers a valuable
timeline of the history of science education in the
United States.

Craig, Gerald S. *Science for the Elementary School
  Teacher*. 5th ed. Waltham, Mass.: Blaisdell, 1966.

  The author addresses teachers on their responsi-
bility to adapt the wonders of science to children's
interests and capabilities. Some of the issues discussed are: content learning vs. process in science
teaching, how basic patterns of the universe and
nature relate to concept formation, the importance
of interaction in science teaching, the place of
science in a democracy, and how the environment
near the school can contribute to science teaching.
The major part of the book focuses on the content of
science: earth, the universe, life on earth, energy
of the universe. In the last 100 pages, the author
offers examples of good science teaching. He classifies concepts and content by grade as they relate to
the book. A teacher will find useful the differences
in teaching methods suggested for each grade and the
emphasis on children's development and level of interest.

DeVito, Alfred, and Gerald Krockover. *Creative
  Sciencing--A Practical Approach*. 2nd ed. Boston,
  Mass.: Little, Brown, 1980.

  This book is concerned with creative methods of
teaching of science. The book is divided into six
chapters with titles that suggest the immediacy of
the topic. Chapter One, "Setting the Stage," addresses teachers' attitudes towards science and
gives an overview of teaching methods that incorporate these attitudes. At times, the style is anecdotal, which helps to identify the authors' viewpoints. Chapter Two presents the conditions for
creative science teaching, which presuppose flexibility, openness to individual interests and differences, good questioning strategies, and receptive-
ness to new technology, e.g., computers. Chapter
Three addresses curriculum and emphasizes the integration of process skills and content, using a
variety of strategies and materials. Chapter Four
encourages teachers to incorporate other subjects

to revise teaching, and Chapter Five confronts the
logistics of daily teaching: how to organize activities, where to order materials, safety, field trips,
special education, etc. Finally, Chapter Six explores creative strategies for evaluations. The
authors pause for questions to the reader and provoke
thinking on how to involve children in the scientific
process. Each chapter ends with a summary that helps
to focus on the issues. This book is accompanied by
"Creative Sciencing Ideas and Activities for Teachers
and Children."

Diamond, Dorothy. *Introduction and Guide to Teaching*
Primary Science. Milwaukee, Wis.: McDonald-Raintree,
1979.

This book was written as an introduction to the
ten books of the Macdonald Educational Series, begun
in Great Britain as a project sponsored jointly by
the Nuffield Foundation and the Social Science Research Council. It aims to assist non-science
teachers with concrete suggestions on how to explore
science teaching. The author encourages an inter-
active-integrative approach where children are involved at their own cognitive and interest levels.
Although it is not a how-to book, it offers suggestions for activities, materials, and environments.
Most of all it encourages teachers to encourage
children in a wide range of interesting experiences
that will help them develop investigative skills
utilizing a variety of resources (books, materials,
media, and the environment at large). This book
will be most helpful to the teacher who is preparing
to use any of the MacDonald series books for science
teaching.

Educational Development Corporation. *The ESS Reader*.
Newton, Mass.: Educational Development Corporation,
1970.

This book discusses the rationale for the development of the Elementary Science Study Curriculum.

The contributors to this reader support the active involvement of children in their learning of science and respect children's findings. Their philosophy on teaching shaped the ESS (Elementary Science Study) Program and the articles remain classics in the literature of how children learn effectively from their environment. Teachers with child-centered approaches to teaching will find these articles inspirational and supportive of an active science teaching approach.

Edwards, Clifford, and Robert L. Fisher. *Teaching Elementary School Science: A Competency Based Approach*. New York: Praeger, 1977.

The book's outstanding feature is its organization of what a teacher must know in order to teach elementary school science. The authors represent a competency based teaching view and provide a wide range of viewpoints on learning theories, behavioral objectives, teaching strategies, content organization, process skills, and evaluation techniques. The book includes a chapter on teaching simulation. Preservice and inservice teachers will want to utilize the exercises provided in the book for self-evaluation. It is a book that concerns itself more with *how* to teach than *what* to teach.

Esler, William K., and Mary K. Esler. *Teaching Elementary Science*. 3rd ed. Belmont, Calif.: Wadsworth, 1981.

A book on elementary school science that can be a textbook for teachers on "what" and "how" to teach science to children. Section One includes conceptual frameworks from all the areas that contribute to effective science teaching, i.e., children's levels of cognitive development (Piaget); behavior learning levels (Gagné); methods of sequencing the inquiry process as well as the content of science; strategies on how to integrate science with other subjects; curriculum theory; criteria on how to choose programs and textbooks followed by brief descriptions of the well-known funded programs of the N.S.F.

Section Two is most of the book and contains chapters on living, physical, and earth sciences. Each area of content is followed by process skills and suggested activities. The grade level is designated for each activity and the appendices are helpful resources for teachers. A well-organized and clearly written sourcebook for teachers in science education.

Gega, Peter C. *Science in Elementary Education*. 4th ed. New York: Wiley, 1982.

This book helps teachers to understand the subject matter, to develop science concepts from phenomena and materials around them, and to plan strategies to teach these concepts to children. The first part of the book addresses issues such as children's learning, inquiry and science teaching, open and closed activities, resources for science teaching, mainstreaming special students, learning centers, and evaluation models. The second and lengthier part concentrates on the content of science and on strategies for teaching it to children. It differentiates between activities and investigations, incorporating problem solving with the latter.

The book is lively and rich in illustrations and diagrams. At the end of each chapter is a listing of appropriate trade books, differentiated by topic and grade level. The book contains a thorough professional bibliography and a special section on animal requirements for survival in science centers. Teachers both preservice and inservice will find this book most helpful because it offers valuable information on science for them as well as for children.

George, Kenneth D., Maureen Dietz, Eugene C. Abraham, and Miles A. Nelson. *Elementary School Science: Why and How*. Lexington, Mass.: Heath, 1974.

The book views the teaching of science as a decision-making process. The decisions concern curricular, instructional and evaluation issues. In the curricular part of the book, the critical factors that influence decisions are learners' developmental stages and the nature of the science program. The instructional issues involve teaching tactics and strategies for which the authors offer helpful explanations and examples. Models of different teaching tactics (initiating, focusing, terminating) are clearly stated. Strategies are considered as choices teachers make to achieve an objective while they utilize certain tactics. Finally, decisions on evaluation are discussed. This book contributes greatly to the understanding of the teaching process and offers guidelines to preservice and inservice teachers on how to structure lessons and programs in science.

Goldberg, Lazer. *Children and Science*. New York: Scribner's, 1970.

This book aims to sensitize adults to the value of science education for children. It addresses parents and teachers and promotes the notion that science education is not a separate entity, but must be integrated into the children's environment wherever they are engaged in learning. Dr. Goldberg discusses the value of science education as a contributor to the development of children's thinking processes and provides many suggestions for adults (teachers, parents) on how to enhance the values of this education. Finally, the author warns that testing is a contradiction of the very goals of the philosophy of science learning. The bibliography offers a wide selection of works for children and adults that reinforce his viewpoints.

A very inspiring book for adults who are concerned that children understand and appreciate science.

Good, Ronald G. *How Children Learn Science: Conceptual Development and Implications for Teaching.* New York: Macmillan, 1977.

This book models science teaching on Piagetian developmental theory. Concept development in science is related to the developmental stages of children and their notions of causality. The experimental interview is recommended as an effective strategy to determine a child's cognitive level and his understanding about causality in physical phenomena. Obviously, such an outlook has implications for a science curriculum, and concrete investigations are presented for various developmental stages, designating expected learning outcomes.

This is not a "how to teach book" but one that utilizes research findings on Piagetian theory and children's thinking and develops a methodology for science teaching. Teachers will find this book very challenging in its approach to cognitive development and children's notions of causality, how such notions differ from one age to another, and what implications they have for science activities. Parts 4 and 6 respectively present science concepts and children's thinking at different levels, and ideas that help children learn science. Documented research findings throughout the book strengthen the position of the author.

Harlan, Jean. *Science Experiences for the Early Childhood Years.* 3rd ed. Columbus, Ohio: Merrill, 1983.

The rationale of this book lies in the assumption that young children's natural interest in knowing the physical world around them motivates them to engage in meaningful science experiences. This rationale helps teachers to plan and teach science to young children. Throughout the book, the science concepts to be taught are followed by planned activities--experiences for children that are enhanced by suggested integrative activities from the areas of art, math, body movement, music and social

studies. This method encourages teachers who may
not feel comfortable with science to get involved
through other topics where they may feel more comfortable. The topics explored are: plant life,
animal life, human body, care and nourishment, air,
water, seasons and weather, rocks and minerals,
magnets, simple machines, sound, light, and electricity. Appendices I and II offer references to
music, poetry, body movement, and science materials.
Each topic is accompanied by a valuable bibliography
of related children's books and extensive reading
for teachers.

Hausman, Howard Y. *Choosing a Science Program for the
Elementary School*. Washington, D.C.: Council for
Basic Education, 1976.

This monograph states the case for science education in elementary schools. The author offers examples from a wide selection of textbooks based on
teaching and hands-on experience in science and
discusses their differences. The N.S.F.-funded
science programs (ESS, S-APA, SCIS, COPES, Minnemast)
are discussed as the hands-on science programs, and
the importance of inservice teacher training for
effective implementation is emphasized. A concise
document with essential information for school
administrators who decide on science programs for
the elementary school.

Henson, Kenneth T., and Yank Delman. *Elementary
Science Methods*. New York: McGraw-Hill, 1984.

The authors aim to acquaint teachers with "everything" that is involved in teaching science to
children in elementary school. The book is useful
as a reference for teachers in elementary school
science. Part I discusses issues that relate to
science teaching, i.e., why science for children;
the nature of science; theories that contribute to
our understanding of children's learning; theories
on the planning and implementing of science teaching;

and writing, objectives, and the evaluation of children's performance. Chapters 7 and 8 are particularly useful for their wide variety of resources and suggestions both for the actual practice of science teaching and for the integration of other curriculum areas (math, art, etc.) into science activities. Parts II, III, and IV are science content sections on life, earth, and physical science respectively. These sections include activities grouped for primary and intermediate grades.

Each chapter is well organized but highly concentrated in concepts for the novice in science teaching. The rich range of suggested resources at the end of each chapter can contribute to the development of a library of children's and teachers' books that will enhance the teaching of science.

Hochman, Vivienne, and Mildred Greenwald. *Science Experiences in Early Childhood Education*. 6th ed. New York: Bank Street Publications, 1969.

This book on science for preschool children continues to be correct in its assumptions on how young children learn science and what are appropriate materials and strategies to enhance such learning. The focus is on young children's science experiences rather than on experiments. The book offers a wide variety of suggested activities that can be integrated into children's lives providing dynamic growth. At present, most preschool programs incorporate such strategies in teaching science to children, so this book continues to be valuable for teachers and parents of preschool children.

Holt, Bess, and Gene Holt. *Science with Young Children*. Washington, D.C.: N.A.Y.E.C., 1977.

This is a comprehensive book on how young children learn science. It discusses the broad role of science in the development of the child, relates the process skills of science to children's investigative capabilities, and identifies children's natural

curiosity as a motivating force for the exploration
of materials and phenomena. The author offers concrete suggestions to teachers on how to develop
environments, suggest activities, and guide experiences in science for children. At all times the
planning of science activities takes into account
children's developmental needs. The element of
safety in teaching science is discussed and the
valuable appendix on common poisonous plants should
be in everybody's possession, especially those who
take nature walks with children.

Humphrey, James H. *Teaching Elementary Science
Through Motor Learning*. Springfield, Ill.: Thomas,
1975.

   Science education through motor activity is one
theory on how to teach science concepts effectively
to children in the elementary grades. The author
explains the nature of physical education activities
and their importance to concept learning. He claims
support for his views from historical sources which
range from Plato (380 B.C.) to L.P. Jacks (1932).
There are lesson plans that illustrate how science
concepts can be played out through motor activities,
and the author emphasizes their particular value
for slow learners. Teaching science through motor
learning should not be confused with active learning
in science, which is a widely accepted format in
the teaching of science concepts. For example, in
teaching the concept that "electricity is the flow
of electrons in a closed circuit" through motor
learning strategies, the children simulate the closed
circuit with their bodies and use a ball to represent the current of flow of electrons. On the other
hand, in an environment where active learning takes
place, the children may use batteries and bulbs to
understand the closed circuit concept.

Hurd, Paul Dehart, and James J. Gallagher. *New Directions in Elementary Science Teaching*. Belmont,
Calif.: Wadsworth, 1968.

The focus of this book are descriptions of thirteen elementary science programs funded by the N.S.F., the U.S. Office of Education, and several private foundations. The programs described are: COPES, S-APA, ESSP (Berkeley), ESSP (Illinois), ESSP (Utah State), ESS, IDP, ISCS, Minnemast, SSCP, SCIS, SQAIESS, and WIMSA. Each program is described in a comprehensive manner and includes instructional materials, desirable learning outcomes, sample lessons, and conditions for successful implementation. The book is a valuable reference for teachers (preservice and inservice) and school administrators, and a note to parents further expands its usefulness. The appendices provide reference information and addresses for each program.

Ivany, J.W. George. *Today's Science; A Professional Approach to Teaching Elementary School Science.* Chicago: Science Research Associates, 1975.

Professionalism in the teaching of science has a special meaning in this book. The author equates professionalism with decision-making and eclecticism on the "whats" and "hows" of teaching science to children. The emergence of professionalism in science teaching has to do with pedagogical methods, "flexibility in style," and a personal philosophy based on sound concepts of science and the nature of learning. Each chapter addresses an issue that relates to the teaching of science (nature of science, children, learning models of teaching, and more) and concludes with a summary of the key concepts discussed and a series of exercises testing the teacher's capabilities in decision-making on the issues discussed. The style is direct and concise and the arguments on professionalism for teachers are consistent throughout the text. The author exhibits the same openness to other views and sustains an unbiased viewpoint in the decision-making exercises. The book will interest teachers and school administrators as a model for decision-making and in choosing a curriculum in science.

Jacobson, Willard, and Abby Baroy Bergman. *Science for Children: A Book for Teachers*. Englewood Cliffs, N.J.: Prentice-Hall, 1980.

The authors present a comprehensive view of teaching for preservice and inservice teachers in elementary science education. In Part I they support the views that science teaching for children must go beyond the classroom and become part of their daily lives. They discuss extensively how teaching science can help children in perceptual development, logical and formal thinking, language skills, and math development. It can also offer special benefits to the handicapped. The role of the teacher is emphasized throughout the book and a competency-based teacher education program in elementary school science is organized in the Appendix. Part II presents science background for the teacher so that the activities suggested will reflect teacher understanding of both the content and the process of science. An extensive bibliography follows each chapter, and services are classified for teachers and for younger and older children.

Jacobson, Willard J., and Harold E. Tannenbaum. *Modern Elementary School Science: A Recommended Sequence*. New York: Columbia University Press, 1961.

The authors respond to the question, "What is science?" in terms of the elementary school. They recommend a two-dimensional program: a "flexible dimension" that relates science to everyday life and other subjects of the curriculum, and a "planned dimension" where high-quality experiences in science are proposed as part of the science program. The recommended sequence in planning a science program is the focal point of the book. The authors take into consideration goals, characteristics, and criteria for planning a program. They suggest that content areas from all fields of science offer strategies in the organization and teaching of the program. They further propose materials and facili-

ties and expand on evaluation guidelines. This
book is a forerunner of later books on the planning
of science programs in the elementary schools.

Kambly, Paul E., and John E. Suttle. *Teaching Elementary School Science Methods and Resources.* New
York: The Ronald Press, 1963.

This book utilizes a traditional methods approach
and represents the attitudes and science teaching
styles that prevailed prior to the 1960s. It is
precise, filled with valuable science information,
and can be used as a resource by teachers who may
want additional ideas on initiating and developing
field, experimental, and culminating activities in
various areas of science.

Karplus, Robert, and Herbert D. Thier. *A New Look at
Elementary School Science.* Chicago: Rand McNally,
1967.

A most valuable book for users of the SCIS curriculum in elementary science. It offers a historical
sequence of the development of the project, incorporates the new visions in science teaching that the
program reflects, and is useful to students in
science education who wish to learn about the exemplary elementary science programs of the 1960s
and their part in the teaching of science to children. The book offers no frills in appearance, but
it is a classic in content.

Kuslan, Louis I., and Harris A. Stone. *Readings on
Teaching Children Science.* Belmont, Calif.: Wadsworth, 1969.

This book incorporates a wide range of viewpoints
on elementary science for children. Thirty-nine
articles fall into the categories: goals of science,
natures of science and children, curriculum objectives and instructional strategies, evaluation,

models in teacher preparation and teaching science
to children. The contributors are well known in
the fields of child development, curriculum, and
science education. Most of the articles document
research and findings that clarify many assumptions
made on the teaching of science to children. The
style varies, but the articles are brief and focused
and present assumptions, data, and conclusions on
science teaching that will interest administrators
and teachers of science in elementary schools.

————. *Teaching Children Science: An Inquiry Approach.* Belmont, Calif.: Wadsworth, 1968.

This book introduces the reader to the history of
inquiry teaching. It offers a historical overview
(100 years of elementary school science) which is a
welcome addition to the evaluation of the inquiry
process in teaching science. It includes all the
well-known elementary science programs of the 1960s
and discusses a wide range of factors that contribute
to effective inquiry-based teaching. However, the
book is not helpful to newcomers in science teaching
because it is only towards the end that the authors
offer applications of inquiry teaching through actual science experiments.

Landsdowne, Brenda, Paul Blackwood, and Paul Brandwein.
*Teaching Elementary Science Through Investigation
and Colloquium.* New York: Harcourt Brace Jovanovich,
1971.

This book presents one of the most comprehensive
analyses of the inquiry method in science teaching.
The authors succeed in interweaving theory and practice through examples that include conversations
between teachers and children during actual science
teaching. Inquiry in teaching science responds to
children's developmental needs and encourages involvement at all stages. Materials play a major
role and children "mess around" during initial discoveries and then are encouraged to discuss their

findings, which in turn contributes to concept development. The teacher is a key factor through the
entire process and evaluation is ongoing and systematic, based on observation techniques and not on
pencil and paper tests. Furthermore, structured
textbook science programs that dictate objectives
and goals in science learning are viewed unfavorably.
Teachers and administrators will find strong arguments in this book in favor of a more open-discovery
colloquium method for teaching science to children.

Lewis, Jane E., and Irene C. Potter. *The Teaching of
Science in the Elementary School.* 2nd ed. Englewood Cliffs, N.J.: Prentice-Hall, 1970.

In this book, the goal of science teaching is the
practice of process skills which lead to the understanding of the content of science. Some helpful
suggestions are offered on how to integrate science
in other areas of the curriculum and how to order
materials for a science program. The major part of
the book is devoted to the content of science (earth,
physical, life sciences). Chapters 6 through 48
are organized theoretically and in conceptual frameworks. Each chapter includes leading questions that
encourage the practice of process skills. The book
is rich in science concepts and investigations and
teachers with some science background will appreciate
it even more than those without. The book is inter-
jected with topics on technology and encourages
scientific investigation on subjects like radioactivity and space flight. Although several investigations are appropriate for young children (6 to 8),
the focus of the teaching is the higher elementary
grades.

McIntyre, Margaret. *Early Childhood and Science: A
Collection of Articles Reprinted from Science and
Children.* Washington, D.C.: N.S.T.A., 1984.

A book that addresses the increasing demands for
preschool science. It represents a wide documenta-

tion of work with young children and science and
includes articles on how children learn, teaching
strategies, and practical experiences with children.
It is of special interest to teachers and parents
of young children. Indeed, a much needed and welcome contribution to early childhood education.

Navarra, John Gabriel, and Joseph Zaffaroni. *Science
in the Elementary School: Content and Methods*.
Columbus, Ohio: Merrill, 1975.

The authors employ the inquiry method to help the
reader investigate the content of their work. The
first part of the book examines the meaning of
science in elementary education and states guidelines for curriculum, resources, and strategies for
teaching. The remaining and longer part offers a
broad spectrum of science and teaching suggestions.
The areas of science are organized into: 1. air-
weather-flight, 2. space-time and earth, and 3. mat-
ter-energy-life. Each chapter states its objectives
for what content must be learned and is followed by
a section with more objectives for how to teach it
to children. The teaching objectives incorporate
process skills, discussion field trips and other
curriculum areas when necessary. The book is a
valuable reference for teachers who feel comfortable
with science and the inquiry process.

Pitz, Albert, and Robert Sund. *Creative Teaching of
Science in the Elementary School*. Boston, Mass.:
Allyn and Bacon, 1974.

The authors present an overview of the history of
science education and argue that present science
teaching will become more effective if elements of
creativity are incorporated in curricula and strategies. This approach offers a great opportunity
for teachers and children to "unleash their creative abilities and become richer individuals."
Science beyond the classroom--at home, in museums
and libraries--is discussed. Studying the lives

and works of well-known scientists also contributes
to creative science learning. The curriculum reform
of the 1960s is reviewed as it relates to the role
of creativity and concrete examples clarify and
demonstrate this point of view. The style is enthusiastic, inspirational, and convincing, and a
selective bibliography on creativity encourages
teachers to read further.

Renner, John W., and William Ragan. *Teaching Science
in the Elementary School*. New York: Harper & Row,
1968.

The authors support the idea that children's developmental stages determine the learning of concepts and claim that an understanding of science is
basic to children's ability to think. The book is
unique in its modeling of science teaching on inquiry
that combines process skills (observing, measuring,
interpreting and so forth) with essential concepts
in science (matter, space, time, energy, change,
etc.). The N.S.F. programs are discussed with
reference to established criteria on the role of
the teacher and learning environment and the book
concludes with evaluation models. The appendices
are unique and include case studies of famous scientists, methods of organizing data collection, and a
cognitive analysis for levels of thought. The book
should be of great interest to experienced science
educators and curriculum developers in general.

Roche, Ruth L. *The Child and Science: Wondering, Exploring, Growing*. Washington, D.C.: Association
for Childhood Education International, 1977.

This monograph offers a convincing rationale for
why young children should get involved in science.
The author uses vignettes that describe both children's science experiences and the concept formations
that children develop through these activities.
This book will encourage any hesitant teacher of
young children (preservice or inservice) to get

involved in science teaching. It is brief, clear, and to the point and the inserted poetry makes it inspirational.

Romey, William D. *Confluent Education in Science.* New York: Ash Lad Press, 1976.

The term "confluent education" encompasses the affective as well as the cognitive aspects of education. In this case the term refers to the integration of language arts, humanities, etc. with science. The book offers examples of instances where "confluent" approaches maximize science learning and strengthen the assumption that motivation is directly linked to learning. Teachers will be encouraged to incorporate science into their overall curriculum. The style is clear, enthusiastic and convincing.

————. *Inquiry Techniques for Teaching Science.* Englewood Cliffs, N.J.: Prentice-Hall, 1968.

This book is organized in two parts. The first part introduces the idea of the active learning of issues related to science teaching (concept formation, teaching strategies, inquiry) and the importance of developing a personal style of teaching. Each topic begins with an activity that involves the readers and follows with criteria that assist them in evaluating their responses. The second part of the book is comprised of articles from well-known scholars in the fields of learning, science education, curriculum development, and evaluation. The viewpoints presented reflect diversity. The book succeeds in challenging teachers of science to reexamine their teaching styles and/or develop new ones based on a better understanding of what teaching science to children is really all about.

Rowe, Mary Budd. *Teaching Science as a Continuous Inquiry: A Basic.* 2nd ed. New York: McGraw-Hill, 1978.

Science teaching is here viewed as synonymous with scientific literacy and relates to contemporary issues such as pollution, food, energy, etc. In the view of the author, science is basic and the implications of what students learn go beyond the level of factual knowledge to include language, logic development, and attitude formation. She makes strong arguments in favor of her philosophy. The writing combines an inquiry-based orientation with a humanistic style that includes a wide range of anecdotes that effectively connect theoretical constructs to practical learning. One example of such effort is Chapter 2, titled "Go Fly a Kite," which demonstrates how the experience of flying a kite can be planned and implemented to enlist a wide range of learning for children in all of the curriculum areas (language arts, math, art, science, social studies). The entire book emphasizes how science process skills and concepts are essential to science learning. The ways in which school environments and teacher roles can enhance inquiry-oriented science are discussed, and considerations are extended to management of group learning, logistics in using manipulators, variables for teaching the handicapped, and types of evaluation. Furthermore, the implications of science learning in the context of the problems of everyday living are recognized (ecological examination of populations, pollution). The book will spark the imagination of the teacher who wants to look at science teaching beyond the isolated lesson plans and the limits of the behavioral objectives that science curricula usually offer.

Sund, Robert B., and Roger W. Bybee. *Becoming a Better Elementary Science Teacher: A Reader*. Columbus, Ohio: Merrill, 1973.

The authors aim to expand teachers' capabilities beyond the teaching of the subject matter. They discuss issues of motivation and learning, special children, the art of questioning, all aspects of curriculum development, affective objectives, diverse views on evaluation, and the role of discovery and inquiry in science teaching. Teachers will find this reader helpful in developing their own viewpoints on how to teach science, as well as other subjects, effectively.

Tannenbaum, Harold E., Nathan Stillman, and Albert Piltz. *Science Education for Elementary School Teachers*. 2nd ed. Boston: Allyn and Bacon, 1966.

The idea that teachers are the critical factor in effective science teaching is a focal point of this book. Curriculum is discussed in conjunction with children's development and levels of interest. Among other topics discussed are: the development of science concepts, the planning of science lessons, the conditions for science teaching, and models of evaluation.

Thier, Herbert D. *Teaching Elementary School Science: A Laboratory Approach*. Lexington, Mass.: D.C. Heath, 1970.

A laboratory-centered approach to science teaching is the focal point of this book. The life sciences are organized as a study of organisms viewed in their complexity, organization, and interrelationships with their environments; and the physical sciences as an explanation of matter—its structure and properties as part of a system, and energy as evidence of interaction within the system. These viewpoints are also reflected in the organization of SCIS (Science Curriculum Improvement Study) to whose development the author has contributed.

The author goes on to discuss learning from a developmental viewpoint, learning environments inside and outside the classroom, and the role of the teachers and evaluations.

A valuable book for preservice and inservice teachers, science curriculum developers, and most of all for users of the SCIS curriculum.

Trojcak, Doris A. *Science with Children*. New York:
McGraw-Hill, 1979.

The author explains to teachers how to comprehend
science, how to help children discover the wonders
of the natural world, and how to develop the conditions so that both these things can occur. All
this appears as a direct dialogue with teachers that
presents to them a range of possibilities on how to
sharpen their decision-making abilities through
skills learned in science and how to adapt strategies
to their styles of teaching. Part I explores science as content and process and discusses how it can
be adapted to children's learning capabilities.
Piaget's theories and tasks on conservation are
discussed and illustrated in detail. Part II combines the teaching of science skills with child-
centered elements. Many exemplary activities illustrate how this can occur. Part III challenges
the teacher to utilize science skills to develop
instructional strategies and implement science
teaching. Finally, the teacher is shown how to
analyze the existing science curricula--S-APA, SCIS,
ESS--and evolve a philosophy and a course of action
most appropriate to his own teaching style and to
children's levels of development and interest. The
book offers inspiration to preservice and inservice
teachers to become thinkers and decision makers and
not just consumers of existing curricula in science.

Vessel, M.F. *Elementary School Science Teaching*.
Washington, D.C.: Center for Applied Research in
Education, Inc., 1963.

This monograph focuses on issues in elementary
school science in the early 1960s. The author develops a logical, historically aware sequence of
arguments on the nature of science education and
traces the making of science curriculum. The book
concludes with a chapter on "Development and Trends"
that incorporates the "new" guidelines presented by
the AAAS (American Association for the Advancement
of Science). Professor Vessel offers an insight on

how thinking in elementary science education began
to change in the early 1960s.

Victor, Edward. *Science for the Elementary School.*
4th ed. New York: Macmillan, 1980.

This is a classic methods book in the teaching of
elementary science. It is divided into two parts.
Part I includes learning theories, children's developmental stages, and how they influence the teaching
of science. Objectives in elementary science curricula and strategies for implementation are discussed. Important methodology in classroom teaching
is presented and a wide range of sample teaching and
resource units are offered, with an overview of possible materials to be used in the classroom. Evaluation models conclude the first part of the book.
Part II, the largest section, focuses on the content
of science and is divided into living things, earth,
and physical sciences. Each chapter is followed by
a list of appropriate activities and a bibliography.
This mammoth favorite is in its fourth edition and
will mainly interest preservice teachers who will
appreciate a structured approach to the teaching of
science with a wide range of diagrams, drawings of
materials, experiments, and helpful appendices.

Victor, Edward, and Marjorie S. Lerner. *Readings in
Science Education for the Elementary School.* 3rd ed.
New York: Macmillan, 1975.

A comprehensive view of science education. The
selected readings reflect the thinking of well-known
writers in science education and related fields and
represent a wide range of viewpoints. The book is
divided into eight sections. The role of science in
the elementary school appears in Section One, including a position statement on NSTA. Section Two
explains theories of intellectual development and
learning, featuring Piaget, Bruner, and Gagné. A
wide range of objectives in elementary science are
discussed in Section Three. Elementary science pro-

grams are reviewed in Section Four. Section Five
offers a variety of approaches to classroom teaching,
including the development of questioning skills,
team teaching, and the unit as a science teaching
strategy. Section Six elaborates on evaluation,
and Section Seven on the planning and creating of
materials and facilities. The last section devotes
considerable space to the training of science teachers and the role of administrators and science super-
visors.

Washton, Nathan Seymour. *Teaching Science in Elementary and Middle Years.* New York: McKay, 1974.

The book offers guidelines on how to study science
education for personal development and how to apply
that learning in the teaching of science to children.
Part I incorporates the components that prepare one
for science teaching—philosophy, psychology methods
of teaching—with a detailed analysis of objectives
and macro/micro lesson planning, criteria for
choosing science curricula, recommendations on how
to teach individuals and groups, and instruction on
how to incorporate evaluation. Part II details a
chronological sequence in the teaching of science
concepts from kindergarten to eighth grade. The
remainder of the book explores the various categories
of science: living, air, water, weather, earth,
matter, energy, electricity, magnets, heat, sound
and light. The style is direct, precise, and traditional in its approach. It is exceptionally rich
in activity ideas, and the differentiation of
teaching methods for each grade level will be helpful to new teachers.

Waters, Barbara. *Science Can Be Elementary: Discovery-
Action Programs for K-3.* New York: Citation Press,
1973.

This book offers a comprehensive overview of the
N.S.F.-funded elementary science programs of the
1960s, i.e., ESS, SCIS, COPES, S-APA, and Minnemast.

It examines them as they relate to concept building, process skills, and content, but most of all as they support child-centered approaches in teaching. The author favors a developmental-interaction approach to teaching and encourages teachers to use children's natural curiosity to get them involved in science, and to be open and flexible to outcomes. The author maintains an informal and direct style, provides teachers with science activities, and encourages them to get involved in science teaching. The Appendices offer a wide selection of professional information on resources for teaching science, e.g., supplies, bibliography, and organizations.

Chapter 2

SCIENCE ACTIVITIES BOOKS

Introduction

Science activities books are written primarily
for the adults who engage children in science learning.
Most authors assume a hands on approach to science
learning and encourage children's involvement. However, there is a considerable difference in pedagogy
on how to teach science effectively to children which
in turn influences learning outcomes. These differences are based on assumptions on how young children
learn most effectively, whether science is taught as
a process or with an emphasis on content, whether
learning outcomes are prescribed by the teacher or
are child-directed, and whether science activities
are integrated in the curriculum of the early childhood program or not.

How Children Learn Science Effectively

One of the criteria used to evaluate the activities books is the viewpoint of the author on how
children learn science effectively. In general, the
authors do not expand on learning theories and children's developmental stages, but some do suggest

developmental guidelines on how to involve children
in science learning while others do not. For example,
in *Experiences in Science for Young Children* by Donald
B. Newman,[1] the author's guidelines on how to involve
children in the activities are based on knowledge
about child development and behavioral objectives.
The author guides the educator through the thinking
process of children and assists him in organizing the
activities so children can adapt their learning according to their developmental stages and to well-
defined objectives.

In other books, such as *Experiments with Everyday
Objects: Science Activities for Children, Parents and
Teachers* by Kevin Goldstein-Jackson,[2] the author does
not base the activities upon developmental guidelines
but presents them with directions for what to do as
children reach the desirable outcomes. They are more
like recipes with clearly stated learning outcomes
and do not indicate for which age group they would
be most appropriate.

The majority of the books present an eclectic
viewpoint in which developmental differentiations
determine a wide range of science activity.

Process vs. Content of Science

Another area where science activity books differ
is in how science ought to be organized for teaching
purposes. As mentioned in Chapter One, Robert Gagné,
who has influenced the organization of science materials
for teaching, considers the process of scientific research essential to the teaching of science to children. This view influences the authors of many science
activities books while others focus their writings on
the content of science.

In the books influenced by scientific inquiry,
children confront problems and the authors assist
them in finding solutions through the scientific
method of observing, data collecting, communicating,
manipulating objects, hypothesizing, predicting and

In the book *Science on a Shoestring* by Herb Strougin,[3] the emphasis is on the development of scientific skills as a way to understand the content of science. In one activity,[4] children study changes in the environment and rely completely on their skills of observation to collect data on how the shadow of the flag pole in the school yard moves through the day. On the basis of their data collecting, they will hypothesize on and infer the causes of this movement.

In contrast, other books choose content of science as their primary focus. Children engage in making things, probing objects, and learning about physical phenomena by following detailed instructions. One such book, rich in science content, is the all-time favorite *Sourcebook for Science Teaching* by UNESCO.[5] It is carefully constructed to contain activities from all areas of science and each activity demonstrates a concept, principle or phenomenon. For example, a series of experiments is constructed to demonstrate how pumps use air pressure, while in another section simple experiments with everyday things illustrate static electricity. In both cases instructions must be carefully followed so the desirable outcome will prevail.

Whose Learning Outcome?

Another criteria in the review of these books are the goals and objectives of the authors on what the learning outcomes should be. In a book such as the *Sourcebook* of UNESCO, the authors state the learning outcomes for each activity and their goals are that children gain a wide variety of scientific knowledge about objects and phenomena. The authors provide instructions and illustrations so that children are assisted in doing a wide variety of experiments with well defined, desirable outcomes. In other words, a successful conclusion of the experiment must coincide with the learning outcomes suggested in the book.

This approach is in contrast to other books' objectives where the activity itself is the goal and the learning outcomes are more child-defined. The authors of such books emphasize that the child's involvement in the activity be on his terms and not on preconceived learning directives and outcomes based on an adult's viewpoint. That is, a child's involvement in collecting seashells and grouping them in ways he/she feels they belong is more important than the knowledge of what kinds of seashells he/she brings back to the class. A child experiencing the wind through kite flying is more important than identifying the northwesterly direction of the wind and its speed. In *Sharing Nature with Children* by J.B. Cornell, the author suggests that children go "hiking" in the woods on their bellies holding a magnifying glass. He places the emphasis on learning outcomes that originate with children's interests, observations and collections.

However, most of the books reflect a middle of the road approach. The authors define the science content of the activities, introduce a strategy that facilitates the projected learning outcome, but encourages children to further probe the object or phenomena as their interests dictate.

Science, Part of or Separate from the Early Childhood Program K-3?

It is natural for children to seek knowledge and understanding of the world around them. The dilemma that exists is whether the knowledge and the process that produces it should permeate the entire learning experience of the child or whether it should be offered as a separate venture.

There are opposing views on this issue. One view is that the goal of science teaching is valuable learning and should be pursued for its own merit. Another belief holds that the kind of learning that is generated by science should serve as the backbone of the curriculum and be part of all the learning areas.

The controversy on this issue is a result of basic difference in pedagogy. The approach that would keep science a separate learning experience for young children is based on the assumption that scientific knowledge is important for its own sake. It is imperative that children's scientific literacy be treated separately so that children will develop mastery of skills and facts in science such as knowing seashells, dissecting fish and learning the parts and their functions, and so forth.

The other view is that effective learning for children occurs when children experience it as a part of their lives. For example, weather can be taught as part of the daily experience of living and not as an isolated lesson, and fish can be dissected as part of a continuous lifelong experience like visiting an aquarium, the fishmarket, the beach, eating a fish, or reading a story about fish. Furthermore, the scientific process used to find out about things and phenomena is good pedagogy in itself and should permeate the entire curriculum of early childhood programs.

In *Creative Sciencing--A Practical Approach* by Alfred DeVito and Gerald Krockover,[6] the integration of the "spirit of science" into the total curriculum is regarded simply as good teaching. Observation, experimentation, questioning analysis, and interpretation of data are significant tools for all areas of the curriculum.

In summary, the authors that focus on science activities represent a wide range of viewpoints, each with its own eclectic rationale.

NOTES

1. Neuman, Donald B. *Experiences in Science for Young Children.* Albany, N.Y.: Delmar Publishers Inc., 1978.

2. Goldstein-Jackson, Kevin. *Experiments with Everyday Objects: Science Activities for Children, Parents and Teachers.* Englewood Cliffs, N.J.: Prentice-Hall, Inc., 1978.

3. Strougin, Herb. *Science on a Shoestring.* Menlo Park, Calif.: Addison Wesley Publishing Co., 1976.

4. Ibid., p. 46.

5. *UNESCO Sourcebook for Science Teaching.* Paris, France: UNESCO, 1962.

6. DeVito, Alfred, and Gerald Krockover. *Creative Sciencing--A Practical Approach.* Boston, Mass.: Little, Brown Co., 1976.

BIBLIOGRAPHY

Allison, Linda. 1. *The Reasons for Seasons.* 2. *Blood & Guts.* Boston, Mass.: Little, Brown Co., Yolla Bolly Press, 1975.

Two books from a series written for children and adults together by a group of California teachers, writers, and artists. They combine science con-cepts--the earth moves around the sun thus the reason for seasons--with activities that motivate children to observe, get involved in the science aspects of the seasons, and integrate them in their daily lives. For example, under the topic of spring, planting is a major activity accompanied by histori-cal accounts that may interest children. The illus-trations range from diagrams to cartoons and are equally appealing to children and adults. *Blood and Guts,* which follows a similar format, has to do with understanding the body and its functions. These books offer to teachers many possibilities to integrate science in the curriculum creatively and to parents an opportunity to develop activities with their children that will be of interest to both of them.

Althouse, Rosemary, and Cecil Main, Jr. *Science Experiences for Young Children*. New York: Teachers
  College Press, 1975.

   A series of booklets thematically organized with
topics related to children's daily experiences (As
We Grow, Colors, Food, Magnets, Pets, Seeds, and
Wheels). Each booklet includes a rationale for the
topic in its brief introduction. The activities
are explicit and state the concept, questions to
be answered through investigation, materials, procedures, and comments on developmental issues as
they relate to each activity. The illustrations
are indicative of the informality that characterizes
this book. A brief but well-chosen bibliography
concludes each booklet. Packaged in a bright card-
board casing, they are easy to store in the classroom.
A practical resource for teachers of young children.

Arnold, Lois B. *Preparing Young Children for Science:
  A Book of Activities*. New York: Schocken Books,
  1980.

   The activities are based on the COPES science
curriculum and adapted to young (5 to 8 years old)
children's levels of development and interest. The
science concepts refer to properties of things,
measuring, ecology and environments, patterns and
relationships. The content is taken from children's
environments. For example, the chapter "Properties
of Things" includes investigations of properties
such as color, shape, texture, magnetism, and ger-
mination, using the appropriate materials. The
author encourages adults (parents, teachers) to explore along with children the science concepts that
apply to materials and phenomena. A list of related
science books for adults and young children further
enhances the use of this book.

Blackwelder, Sheila Keyser. *Science for All Seasons*.
  Englewood Cliffs, N.J.: Prentice-Hall, Inc., 1980.

The author recommends that the scientific process be used as a way to explore the content of the book and encourages teachers to engage children in open discussions so they may further clarify their investigations and findings. The seasonal approach facilitates the scheduling of science in the school calendar and relates it to curriculum. The content of the book is organized into: Fall (the physical self, anatomy); Winter (frost and snow, electricity, magnets, light and shadows, crystals, rocks, volcanos, dinosaurs and birds); Spring (weather, spring as a season, environment, pollution); Summer (insects, fish, shells, stars). The author supplements each activity with introductory notes to the teacher and extensive readings and bibliography. Each topic combines content with process skills and suggestions to teachers on how to guide children to "get results" and "find out phenomena."

Bowman, Mary Lynne, and Herbert L. Cook. *Recycling Activities for the Classroom*. Columbus, Ohio: ERIC/ SMEAC, Ohio State University, 1978.

This book addresses the environmental issues of recycling as an alternative to increasing the use of natural resources and to reduce solid wastes. The authors have developed activities for students in all grades and classified them accordingly. The format of presentation for each activity includes purpose, grade level, subject matter (science, math, social studies, language arts), references, and the activity itself which incorporates questions to be answered by the students through their investigations. The authors promote teacher initiative and encourage children's decision-making in their involvement and their findings. The thematic emphasis of this book and the valuable appendices of resources make it particularly important and valuable as a tool for environmental education.

Brown, Sam, ed. *Bubbles, Rainbows and Worms--Science Experiments for Preschool Children*. Mt. Rainer, Md.: Gryphon House Inc., 1981.

The author bases the activities of the book on the assumption that children develop science concepts through the knowledge they gain as they investigate the properties of the physical world. In the ten commandments for teaching science to young children, the author emphasizes the need for children to be in charge of the investigations and findings and for teachers to facilitate the process. This popularized recipe-like activities book is easy to follow, includes helpful illustrations, and uses materials that interest children and are easy to obtain. The content is organized along the lines of familiar topics such as: animals, plants, environment, senses, water, and a series of miscellaneous activities that include magnets, food, and wheels. A suggested list of children's books follows each chapter.

Carmichael, Viola S. *Science Experiences for Young Children*. 4th Printing. Sierra Madre, Calif.: S. California Association for the Education of Young Children (P.O. Box 691), 1973.

This typed manual on science experiences is direct and informal in its approach. It emphasizes the scientific method as a way of finding out and requires that children get involved with materials. It integrates art and language throughout the science investigations and offers tips on raising children's interest levels. The topics include: rocks, soil fossils, plants and animals, weather, outer space, day and night, airplanes and rockets, human body, senses, cooking, machines, electricity and magnets. Each unit includes science information for teachers, strategies for teaching, and ideas for class projects that include the arts. A valuable reference for teachers who want to integrate science investigations in the curriculum.

Cobb, Vicki. *Science Experiments You Can Eat.* New
   York: J.B. Lippincott Co., 1974.

   The author focuses on various aspects of cooking
and eating as means of teaching science. For example, she identifies scientific processes such as
experimentation and science concepts such as change
and uses the activity of beating egg whites to stiff
peaks to teach them to children. The book is a
good resource to supplement any science program that
includes nutrition or the exploration of chemistry
concepts in everyday living.

Coon, Herbert L., and Michele Y. Alexander. *Energy
   Activities for the Classroom.* Columbus, Ohio: Ohio
   State University Press, 1976.

   The rationale for these selected energy teaching
activities is based on the urgency of energy problems that have emerged in our world. The authors
urge teachers to involve students in understanding
the science of energy and in exploring the diversity
of solutions on energy issues. Each teaching activity states purpose, grade level (K-12), subject
matter (basically science but other subjects may be
included), concept, and the activity itself. The
authors emphasize the scientific process as a way
of exploring and arriving at solutions to the existing problems. A well-documented and organized resource for teachers.

Cornell, Joseph B. *Sharing Nature with Children.*
   Nevada City, Calif.: Amanda Publications, 1979.

   This modest paperback includes valuable tips and
activities for adults on how to organize nature
walks with children, what experiences to provide,
and how to enhance, share, and enjoy children's
discoveries in the natural world. The author understands how children learn effectively and what interests them. He encourages sensory explorations
like observing smells and sounds and microhiking on

your belly with a magnifying glass. He utilizes
games and simulations to explain life cycles and
animal behaviors. He encourages aesthetic apprecia-
tion along with scientific exploration and enthusi-
astically urges parents and teachers to share nature
with children.

Couchman, T.K., Y.C. MacBean, A. Stecher, and D.F.
Wentworth. *Examining Your Environment*. 12 vols.
Minneapolis, Minn.: Winston Press, 1976.

A series of twelve paperback books written for
teachers who want to teach environmental science
in a creative and effective way. Each book is organized thematically and does not require great
knowledge on the topic by the teacher. Each activity
starts with a question to be investigated and can
be used independently or in a sequence. Children's
interest and age level is considered all through the
books. A bibliography and glossary is found at the
end of each book. All activities are field tested
and the books are illustrated with natural wonders,
children's work, diagrams, and documentation on
children's findings. The very attractive and dynamic
texts will motivate even the most hesitant teacher
to get involved in environmental investigations.
Examining Your Environment Titles: 1. Astronomy;
2. Birds; 3. Dandelion; 4. Ecology; 5. Mapping
Small Plans; 6. Mini-Climates; 7. Running Water;
8. Small Creatures; 9. Snow and Ice; 10. Trees;
11. Your Senses.

DeVito, Alfred, and Gerald H. Krockover. *Creative
Sciencing Ideas and Activities for Teachers and
Children*. 2nd ed. Boston, Mass.: Little, Brown &
Co., 1980.

This book is a natural companion to the author's
book *Creative Sciencing--A Practical Approach*. It
is a resource book organized by activities that emphasize a combination of subject matter and science
skills. The format used to cross-reference the

science skills with the content must be well understood before the book is utilized in science teaching. An understanding of children's developmental
stages is also a prerequisite for teachers so they
may adapt the activities appropriately. The activities are independent of each other, the style of
presentation is original, and many projects incorporate other subjects so that children may better
understand the role of science in their lives and
not treat it as a separate entity. Teachers are encouraged to do their own brainstorming on how to
use the activities more effectively and ideas are
offered on how to motivate the students to get involved.

Section I includes 130 activities and cross-
references them between science skills and subject
matter. Section II provides suggestions on how to
develop resources on a minimum budget. Section III
focuses on techniques such as soldering, setting up
circuits, and so forth. Section IV offers 20 creative recipes that incorporate science concepts but
can be used in other subjects of the curriculum:
pastes, dyes, printing ink, bubble solutions, and
so forth. Appendix A cross-references science activities with other subjects. Conversion tables
and bibliographies follow.

Elementary Science Study. 33 vols. New York: McGraw-
Hill Book Co., 1969.

These activity-centered books represent joint efforts of scientists and teachers from many disciplines with a unified view on how children may learn
science more effectively and enjoyably. Their purpose is to help a teacher to make the classtoom a
laboratory where children can adapt their learning
to their developmental stages and levels of interest.
Content and scientific process are combined in a
flexible scheme where children control their investigations and record their findings, while the teache
facilitates and guides the science study. Each book
can be used independently as well as a resource to

further explore a topic of science. The activity-centered books are listed below according to the area of science study, title of unit, and grade level:

Physical Science: Light and Shadow (K-3), Mobiles (K-4), Spinning Tables (1-2), Mirror Cards (1-6), Sink and Float (2-7), Clay Boats (2-8), Drop Streams & Containers (3-4), Mystery Powders (3-4), Ice Cubes (3-5), Colored Solutions (3-8).

Biological Sciences: Growing Seeds (K-3), Life of Beans & Peas (K-4), Butterflies (K-5), Eggs and Tadpoles (K-6), Animals in Classroom (K-9), Brine Shrimp (1-4), Changes (1-4), Pond Water (1-7), Starting from Seeds (3-7), Mosquitoes (3-9).

Earth Sciences: Daytime Astronomy (1-8), Sand (2-3), Rocks & Charts (3-6), Where Is the Moon? (3-7).

General Skills: Match and Measure (K-3), Primary Balancing (K-4), Pattern Blocks (K-6), Geo Blocks (K-6), A Tangram (K-8), Musical Instrument Recipe Book (K-9), Attribute Games and Problems (K-9), Printing (1-6), Structures (2-6).

George, K.D., M.A. Dietz, and E.C. Abraham. *Science Investigations for Elementary School Teachers.* Boston, Mass.: D.C. Heath Co., 1974.

A supplement to the book by K.D. George et al. The investigations are structured according to specific objective materials to be used and procedures to be followed. The appendixes further clarify for teachers the science concepts and children's learning outcomes. Although the content will interest children of all ages, this book will be most appropriate for children at the higher grades.

Goldstein-Jackson, Kevin. *Experiments with Everyday Objects: Science Activities for Children, Parents and Teachers.* Englewood Cliffs, N.J.: Prentice-Hall, Inc., 1978.

The author seeks to increase the level of interest in science for children and adults through a series

of experiments. The materials used are familiar
and each experiment reflects its own science concept and subject matter. The content is organized
into seven categories: air and water pressure,
buoyancy, surface tension, mechanics, chemistry,
color and candles, viewing and drawing, and electricity and magnetism. Each experiment is illustrated for further clarification and can be used
independently of the others. The variety of experiments is wide and they border on the element of
magic (if you don't know the scientific explanations
that go with them). There is an expected result for
each experiment and the author assumes that understanding will emerge from performance. A resource
for the teacher or parent who knows science and is
looking for experiments to do together with children.

Graf, Rudolf F. *Safe and Simple Electrical Experi-*
     ments. New York: Dover Publications, Inc., 1973.

     A heavily illustrated book on electrical experi-
ments that is easy to follow for teachers, parents,
and children. There are 38 experiments in static
electricity, 31 on magnets, and 31 on current electricity and electromagnetism. The materials used
are simple, safe and easy to find, and the activities
are for children in K-6 grades. Two pages on the
history of discoveries in electricity offer an extra
point of interest for the older children. A valuable
sourcebook for classrooms that engage in the teaching of electricity and magnetism.

Habben, Dorothy. *Science Experiments That Really*
     Work. Chicago: Follett Publishing Co., 1970.

     According to the author, this activity book in-
cludes field tested experiments that have motivated
children to investigate and answer questions on
their own. The activities are organized into seven
parts and include experiments with air, carbon
dioxide, heat, crystals, magnets, electricity, and
sound. Several activities are described in each

category, and each experiment ends with a key question for the child to answer. The illustrated activities can be used independently or as a supplement in other physical science curricula. The materials are simple and easy to find in the everyday environment. A special section "more about each experiment" can assist children to explore further science concepts.

Haldary, D.F., and S.H. Cohen. *Laboratory Science and Art for Blind, Deaf and Emotionally Disturbed Children: A Mainstreaming Approach*. Baltimore, Md.: University Park Press, 1978.

This comprehensive book is based on years of experience in the adaptation of science curricula (SCIS, SAPA and ESS) to the teaching of blind, deaf, and emotionally disturbed children. Appropriate counterpart art activities are proposed that will further enhance the children's development of science concepts. The book is organized into four sections. Section I offers both a convincing rationale why science and art are important in the educational process of handicapped children and information on how to integrate and mainstream them. A helpful chart cross references the science with the art activities. Section II classifies and develops the science activities. Each activity includes exploration by the child, the science concept it teaches, materials and procedures, and adaptation for each handicap. A brief Section III presents useful background on science and material for teachers, and Section IV describes art activities in a way similar to science activities (Section II). This is a most valuable book for preservice and inservice teachers and administrators in elementary education. The 50 science and 63 art lessons are supportive evidence for effective mainstreaming. The illustrators depict children's involvement and strengthen further the authors' views on science and art study for the handicapped.

Herbert, Don. *Mr. Wizard's Supermarket Science*. New
York: Random House, 1980.

The book is based on Mr. Wizard's television show
and focuses on the products of supermarkets and the
science activities that can be generated from them.
The author claims that "functional fixedness" of
objects prevents students from using them creatively.
Thus, he uses products of a supermarket to explore
science concepts. For example, milk-based glue,
vinegar rocket launches, gelatin stalagmites, cereal
box cameras, and so forth. There is an element of
sensationalism in the book but in the hands of a
teacher with science knowledge it can provide creative science explorations for children. Each activity is independent and can supplement any science
program.

Herbert, Don, and H. Ruchlis. *Mr. Wizard's 400 Experiments in Science*. Brooklyn, N.Y.: Book-Lab,
Inc., 1968.

A series of science experiments with diagrams and
detailed directions using materials that are easily
found in our immediate surroundings. This book will
be useful to a teacher who is knowledgeable about
science and wants more experiments and projects to
enrich science teachings.

Hill, Katherine E. *Exploring the Natural World with
Young Children*. New York: Harcourt Brace Jovanovich,
1976.

The author believes that children's exploration
of natural phenomena is as important to their development as other aspects of their preschool experiences. The suggested experiences in science
are grouped into themes such as air, water, cooking,
inside things, light, sound, moving things, our
earth, space, animals, and plants. Each topic includes concepts to be formulated, materials to be
used, procedures to follow, questions for the teacher

to ask and possible children's answers, as well as appropriate age levels. The materials are simple, the style informal and direct, and although there are no illustrations the book is easy to follow.

Hoffman, Helen Marie, and H. and Kenneth S. Ricker. *Sourcebook in Science Education and the Physically Handicapped*. Washington, D.C.: N.S.T.A., 1979.

This publication is the result of a working conference sponsored by the National Science Teachers Association in 1977. It is a valuable sourcebook for teachers who have physically handicapped students in their science classes. The topics discussed are: science education for the handicapped, science for the auditorily, orthopedically, and visually handicapped, and science programs beyond the school. Possible careers in science and related fields are discussed as well as the future implications of science education for the physically handicapped. The sections on the science for the auditorily, orthopedically, and visually handicapped offer valuable background and activities for the teacher. The extensive bibliographies complement each section effectively. The input of so many scholars in this field contribute immensely to the usefulness of this publication.

Hone, Elizabeth B., Alexander Joseph, and Edward Victor. *A Sourcebook for Elementary Science*. 2nd ed. New York: Harcourt Brace Jovanovich, Inc., 1971.

A traditional, comprehensive sourcebook on science and classroom activities written for elementary school teachers. The detailed diagrams and photographs contribute greatly to an understanding of how the extensive science content of the activities works. The book is organized thematically along biological, physical and earth sciences lines and it includes topics of technology such as machines and engines, communications, radioactivity, fibers and clothing, space travel, and flight. Although the scope of the book focuses on science for older children, many of the activities can be adapted for very young children. An extensive bibliography follows each chapter.

Jacobson, Willard, and Abby Bergman. *Science Activities for Children.* Englewood Cliffs, N.J.: Prentice-Hall, Inc., 1983.

This book of science activities is for adults who plan science experiences for children at home, in school, or at camp. The content is organized thematically: plants and animals; air, water and weather; energy (heat, light and solar); studying ourselves; the earth; magnetism and electricity; making and exploring the universe. A brief introduction that includes rationale and instruction precedes the activities of each specific theme. Each activity is independent and is organized with title, age group, type of investigation, materials, procedures, and a section on enrichment. The materials are simple and inexpensive and the authors emphasize the importance of enjoyment and involvement as key components of children's science experiences. A valuable resource for homes and camps and for existing science curriculum in the elementary classroom.

Macdonald Educational Science 5/13. Set I. Milwaukee, Wis.: Macdonald-Raintree, Inc., 1974.

A team effort of British educators, including members of the Nuffield Foundation, has produced a series of books with science topics that children are most likely to want to investigate. They are books for adults who teach children between the ages of 5 and 13. Each book is organized thematically, taking into consideration children's developmental stages, the integration of science in the curriculum, children's interests, investigations, findings and recordings. They are field tested and well-documented with photographs, diagrams and children's readings.

Each book has a chief author and a working team, and can be used independently of the other books in the set. These dynamic, child-centered science teaching books can be helpful to teachers who share the author's views on how children can learn science more effectively.

Science 5/13 titles: 1. Working with Wood, 2. Time, 3. Early Experiences, 4. Structures and Forces (2 volumes), 5. Science from Toys, 6. Minibeasts, 7. Holes, Gaps and Cavities, 8. Metals, 9. Change (2 volumes), 10. Trees, 11. Like and Unlike (2 volumes), 12. Coloured Things, 13. Children and Plastic; *Using the Environment*: 1. Early Experiences, 2. Investigations, 3. Tackling Problems, 4. Ways and Means.

McGavack, John, Jr., and Donald P. LaSalle. *Guppies, Bubbles and Vibrating Objects*. New York: The John Day Co., 1969.

This book offers strategies and science activities to help children have experiences very similar to those of scientists. The authors begin with helpful recommendations on how to motivate children in primary grades to learn science. They offer a wide range of activities accompanied by photographs of children at work that contribute greatly to an understanding of how to interest and involve children in science investigations.

Miles, Betty. *Save the Earth--An Ecology Handbook for Kids*. New York: Alfred A. Knopf, 1974.

The author presents to children a comprehensive view of the earth's ecological problems. She takes into account the integrative way children learn and combines reading skills, value learning, and concept formation throughout the book. The content is organized in sections: land, air, water, and how-to-do-it. Each section begins with an inspiring, informative background and well-chosen illustrations followed by projects that integrate all subjects of

the curriculum. Indeed a well-documented and creatively written ecology handbook for kids.

Milgrom, Harry. *ABC Science Experiments*. New York:
Crowell, 1970.

   A brief, simple, colorful, easy to read series of
26 activities organized in an alphabetical sequence.
It is written and illustrated for children, but an
index of notes at the end of the book addresses
adults and clarifies the science concepts that
emerge from each investigation.

Mitchell, John Hanson. *A Guide to Seasons*. Lincoln,
Mass.: Massachusetts Audubon Society, 1982.

   This booklet is a selection of activities from the
discontinued magazine *The Curious Naturalist* of the
Massachusetts Audubon Society. The activities are
organized by seasons as they appear in the Northern
Hemisphere. They include all of nature's exhibits
such as animals, plants, the stars, and a weekly
calendar of nature's events such as which animals
appear when and what flowers blossom when. It is
heavily illustrated, well-documented, and informally
written. An essential companion to a nature study
that involves adults and children.

Munson, Howard R. *Science Activities with Simple
Things*. Belmont, Calif.: Fearon Publishers Inc.,
1962.

   This book of 29 experiments and 24 demonstrations
was written as a supplement to any existing physical
science program. The author specifies first the
simple things and then designs activities that use
them. The list of materials includes rubber bands,
soda straws, paper clips, paper and plastic cups,
marbles, boxes, pins and needles, and other odds
and ends. The content of the book is divided into
a series of experiments followed by demonstrations.

The experiments are stated in terms of problems to
be solved and include purpose, materials, procedure,
and illustrations. The demonstrations are performed
by teachers or students to explain a science fact
or prove a point. The book will be useful to adults
who understand science concepts and can capitalize
on the availability of simple materials.

Nelson, Leslie, and George C. Lorbeen. *Science Activities for Elementary Children*. 8th ed. Dubuque,
Iowa: Wm. C. Brown Publishers, 1984.

The book includes a very wide selection of activities for children in the elementary grades. The
activities are organized thematically on the basis
of physical, biological, and earth sciences. There
are also interdisciplinary topics such as ecology,
aviation, space travel, health and safety. Each
activity is stated as a problem, followed by recommended procedures and materials. The children's
findings are suggested and the illustrations help
the teacher to organize the investigations. A
classic sourcebook of science actitivies in its 8th
edition.

Nickelsburg, Janet. *Nature Activities for Early
Childhood*. Reading, Mass.: Addison-Wesley, 1976.

The author, a long-time naturalist and educator,
asks adults to "help children see more and not to
obscure their vision with a multitude of facts."
The 44 projects in nature activities are clearly
stated, attractively illustrated, and encourage child
involvement. Each project is independent, considers
children's developmental stages, and provides adults
with background material and vocabulary so they may
facilitate the science experiences for the children.
The focus of the activities are animals, plants,
and non-living things—all of which can be found in
children's natural environments. The content is
divided into various sections such as outdoor group
projects, projects with small animals, indoor projects,

looking for things in the ground, watching things,
and projects with plants. Each section ends with
suggested books for adults and children. A valuable
companion to the science curricula of preschool and
early primary grades.

Redleaf, Rhoda. *Open the Door Let's Explore*. St.
Paul, Minn.: Toys 'n Things Press, 1983.

   This book is a resource for adults (parents,
teachers) who want to maximize young children's
learning through the exploration of their physical
environment. The author cautions adults on young
children's developmental differences, emphasizes
the integration of nature's exploration to the curriculum, elaborates on how learning may occur and
offers tips on how to develop effective walks. Each
walk is independent and includes introductory activities, ideas for exploring, follow-up activities,
language activities, and books for children. An informal, attractive resource book, easy to implement
in any early childhood learning environment.

Riegor, Edythe. *Science Adventures in Children's Play*.
New York: Playschools Assoc., 1968.

   This early pamphlet is sensitive and responsive to
children's levels of interest and cognition. The
science experiences are organized around topics such
as exploring the neighborhood, map making, trees,
birds, rocks and minerals, shadows and weather,
wind, plants, animals, and ideas from here and there.
Each investigation is integrated with other curriculum areas. The content is presented in a narrative form and includes information on the topic,
suggestions on how to get started, how to involve
children, and how to integrate each "adventure in
science" with other curriculum areas. A helpful resource for a non-traditional classroom.

Rights, Mollie. *Beastly Neighbors*. Boston, Mass.: Little, Brown & Co., 1981.

One more book from the series of the Brown Paper School (see *Blood and Guts*, *The Reason for Seasons*). The author explores science in terms of the immediate urban/suburban environments of children. Each chapter is presented as a combination of challenging questions and activities in cartoon drawings using children's jargon. A useful, entertaining resource book for classrooms and homes where adults may want to explore creatively with children their immediate environments--whether it's the supermarket, wasted garbage, bugs, birds, air, rain, or creative gardening.

Rockwell, Robert E., Elizabeth A. Sherwood, and Robert A. Williams. *Hug a Tree*. Mt. Rainier, Md.: Gryphon House, Inc., 1983.

This book gives information to adults (parents, teachers) on how to carry out environmental activities with children 2 to 5 years old. The information includes how to use language effectively and how to help children develop observation skills, identify, group, and record their findings. Furthermore, the logistics on how to organize for an outdoor experience is discussed in detail and is supplemented with a list of books and other resources. Each activity designates age, cost of materials, what to do, and a "want to do more" section. Although each chapter is independent, it is advisable to use them in sequence. A book that is easy to integrate in a child-centered early childhood program.

Russell, Helen Ross. *Small World: A Field Trip Guide*; *Soil: A Field Trip Guide*; *Winter: A Field Trip Guide*. Boston, Mass.: Little, Brown & Co., 1972.

The three books in this series investigate in depth the environments of small living things, soil, and the season of winter respectively. They present

science information along with teaching strategies
for field trips. *Small World* explains habitats of
insects, moss, lichens, etc., and helps teachers to
organize discovery experiences for children outside
the classroom. The content of *Soil: A Field Trip
Guide* details a variety of rocks, minerals, dead
plants and animals, as well as the process of recycling. Ideas for projects on ecology are suggested for students to undertake. The exploration of a
northeastern winter offers information on plants,
birds, insects, ice, snow and other aspects of
nature's behavior during the winter season. A child-
centered approach on how to engage children in investigations underscores the teaching strategy offered in this book. All three books are enhanced
by excellent photographs and illustrations.

————. *Ten Minute Field Trips--A Teacher's Guide.*
Chicago, Ill.: J.G. Ferguson Publishing Co., 1973.

This book is written for children in the primary
grades and its focus is how to study the environment
through ecological field trips on the school/camp
grounds. The book is divided into sections on plants,
animals, interdependence of living things, physical
science, earth science, and ecology. Each section
includes background material on the topic, related
classroom activities, teacher preparation, and field
trip possibilities. Furthermore, listings of field
trips are cross referenced for paved school grounds,
and pictures are used widely to clarify sites and
children's involvement. A widely used book for outdoor education.

Schmidt, Victor E., and Verix Rockcastle. *Teaching
Science with Everyday Things.* 2nd ed. New York:
McGraw-Hill Book Co., 1982.

The authors discuss their views on the importance
of science for children and on the value of counting
and measuring as process skills. Their emphasis is
that process is as important as content; that in

science, affective and cognitive objectives are
equally important; and that materials of daily use
are best suitable for teaching science concepts.
They address teachers with minimum science training
and present them with science knowledge as well as
suitable teaching strategies. The illustrations
enhance the explanations in the text and there is
a categorized bibliography at the end of each chapter. A book that goes beyond the scope of activities
and is a useful resource for teachers.

Sheckles, Mary. *Building Children's Science Concepts.
Experience with Rocks, Soil & Water*. 3rd Printing.
New York: Teachers College, Columbia University,
Bureau of Publication, 1964.

Both a teacher training manual on how to organize
good science teaching and an activities book on how
to investigate the atmosphere, rocks, soil, and
water. The author uses an open narrative style with
suggestions on how children should investigate, discuss, and conceptualize science. A good resource
for earth science curriculum in the primary grades.

Silver, Donald M. *Life on Earth--Biology Today*. New
York: Random House, 1983.

This reference book is particularly valuable for
the colorful, explicit diagrams and excellent pic-
torial information on anatomical issues (the insides
of a rabbit for example) and on nature's processes
such as photosynthesis. The text is equally valuable
to teachers and children in the primary grades.
Plant and animal life is pictorially described with
concrete explanations, and comparisons among organisms are creatively demonstrated. A valuable
addition to any life sciences curriculum.

Sisson, Edith. *Nature with Children of All Ages*.
Englewood Cliffs, N.J.: Prentice-Hall, Inc., 1982.

This book is most suitable to share with children
in exploring nature and teaching the outdoors. The
author emphasizes the affective benefits of outdoors
science investigations and offers concrete suggestions and tips on how to organize and plan these
outings. Science background is offered to the adults
as well as teaching strategies on how to involve
the children. The book is informal, direct, sensitive, and most valuable to teachers, parents, camp
leaders who want to investigate and enjoy nature
with children. Attractive illustrations, informative diagrams, and a useful bibliography for both
adults and children contribute to the effectiveness
of this book.

Sprung, Barbara, M. Froschl, and P.B. Campbell. *What
Will Happen If ... Young Children and the Scientific
Method*. New York: Educational Equity Concepts, Inc.,
1985.

The book emphasizes the importance of math, science, and technology-related activities to the development of young children. The spirit of inquiry
and the equitable access by both sexes underscore
the rationale and the strategies of implementation
for a science program. The activities are organized
around familiar surroundings and materials such as
sand, water, blocks, and familiar machines such as
typewriters. Science concepts to explore are:
comparisons between water and sand; momentum with
ramps and balls using the block area; density, vis-
cosity, using different liquids; and machines at
home and school to explore technology. A brief but
valuable chapter on resources complements this
equitable approach to science experiences for young
children of both sexes.

Stein, Sara. *Great Pets*. New York: Workman Publishing Co., 1976.

An *Extraordinary Guide to Usual and Unusual Family
Pets* is the subtitle of the book and it is the most

appropriate way to describe *Great Pets*. This book
contains valuable information on a wide variety of
animals that could be used as pets in schools and
homes to enhance science teaching about animals.
The author offers a wide variety of possibilities
with tips on cost, food, habitats, care and brief
summaries to help compare one animal with another
in the same category. This information is grouped
in the following categories: pets in the wild; over-
weight pets; vivarium pets; aquarium pets; serpen-
tarium pets; pet birds; pocket pets; unusual apartment
pets; pet cats; and pet dogs. A special section discusses and demonstrates the construction of various
habitats. The illustrations and diagrams enhance
even further this valuable companion to classrooms
and homes that help children to raise and understand
pets.

―――――. *The Science Book*. New York: Workman Publishing Co., 1979.

This unusual book encourages teachers (parents too)
and children to engage in investigations that concern their immediate environments, including themselves. The content is rich in science facts and
ideas for investigation. It is divided into three
sections: outsides, insides, and invisibles. These
unusual categories address the types of investigations in which children may get involved. "Outsides"
includes the behaviors of pests, pets, and people
and deals with topics like flea habits, baby and
toddler behavior, and so forth. "Insides" addresses
aspects of plants and animals that require probing
such as the assembly of chicken skeletons, reproduc-
tive systems, and the nature of "goose pimples."
"Invisibles" focuses on sensory experiences and perception. The investigations can be adapted for a
wide range of ages and can also be integrated in the
curriculum. The style is direct, informal, and the
wide variety of photographs and diagrams contributes
to the artistic appearance of this unusual, creative
science book.

Stronck, David R., ed. *Understanding the Human Body.
Sourcebook III.* Columbus, Ohio: ERIC/SMEAC, Ohio
State University, 1983.

This well-organized sourcebook on the human body,
its functions, health, growth, and development contains 54 field tested activities contributed by
teachers of the elementary grades. The editor presents a convincing rationale for health education
during the elementary schooling of children. The
topics presented are body organs and systems, the
five senses, growth and development, nutrition and
foods, pollution, diseases and drugs, poisons and
safety. The activities for each topic are structured
with a title, focus, background and challenges,
materials and equipment, procedures, and further
challenges and references. Each chapter is independent of the others although a sequenced approach is
recommended. The style is direct and informal and
the activities are easy to implement. A valuable
sourcebook for every classroom teacher.

Strongin, Herb. *Science on a Shoestring.* Reading,
Mass.: Addison-Wesley Publishing Co., 1976.

This book aims to create low cost, high quality
science for the elementary grades. The investigations are grouped around 3 conceptual themes: scientific methods, change and energy, and fields and
forms. Each investigation follows a lesson plan and
includes grade level, specific concept/skill, materials, vocabulary, activity, notes to teacher,
approximate time duration, evaluation and suggestions for extending the investigation at home.
Although each activity is independent of the others,
sequencing is recommended for certain of them, and
the author cautions on differences of children's
responses at different grade levels. The investigations can be integrated easily in a science curriculum where the process approach is essential.

Sund, Robert, B.W. Tillery, and L.W. Trowbridge. *Elementary Science Discovery Lessons: The Biological Sciences*. Boston, Mass.: Allyn and Bacon, Inc., 1970.

The investigations on animals and plants take into account the relationships of the organisms to their environments, their structures and function, and the diversity of type and unity of pattern in living things. Each investigation is organized to include grade level concepts, materials, procedure, teacher's questions for class discussion, and expected answers. A certain amount of background in biological sciences is recommended for the teacher.

Teaching Primary Science. 9 vols. Milwaukee, Wis.: Macdonald-Raintree, Inc., 1978.

These books represent joint efforts of scientists and teachers from many disciplines with a unified view on how children can learn science more effectively and enjoyably. Each book covers a specific topic and contains children's investigations, findings and documentations as well as the teachers' input in the actual teaching. Diagrams and photographs enhance further this valuable series on creative science teaching. The titles of the books in the series are: Candles, Seeds and Seedlings, Paints and Materials, Science from Water Play, Fibres and Fabrics, Mirrors and Magnifiers, Science from Wood, Musical Instruments, and Aerial Models.

Throop, Sara. *Science for the Young Child*. Belmont, Calif.: Fearon Publishers, Inc., 1974.

Although the author refers to this book as a "cookbook" with a variety of recipes to try, in reality it is more than that. A brief (61 pages) but compact collection of science activities that are developmentally appropriate for young children (preschool-early grades) with topics that interest young children: senses, animal and plant life, weather,

rocks, liquids, motion and movement, magnets, simple
machines, and ourselves. Each topic is independent
of the others. Tips are offered to teachers on how
to facilitate children's learning. Interactions with
materials and the articulation of children's findings are important learning objectives in this useful resource book for teachers of young children.

UNESCO Sourcebook for Science Teaching. New York:
UNESCO Publication Center, 1973.

The updated sourcebook on science experiments
focuses on more formal science techniques and assumes that teachers must understand science. Although most of the activities are for older children,
an experienced teacher can adapt some science experiments for children in the early grades. The content
is organized around themes such as: resources, facilities and techniques for science teaching, physical/
biological, and earth/space science. The appendices
include many scientific tables not applicable to the
science learning of young children.

Wheatley, John, and Herbert Coon. *100 Teaching Activities in Environmental Education*. Columbus,
Ohio: Ohio State University, The ERIC Center for
Science, Mathematics and Environmental Education,
1970.

A well-documented resource for teachers of children
of all ages. The color-coded pages divide the book
into grade levels (K-3; 4-6; 7-9; 10-12). Although
the activities address environmental science, other
subject areas are effectively integrated in the investigations. Each activity includes grade level,
subjects (other than science), problems to be investigated, concept, purpose of the activity, references, and the activity itself with tips on how to
enhance further children's learning. The style is
direct and informal, provides excellent organization, and the book is a valuable resource for teachers of environmental education.

Zubrowski, Bernie. *Ball Point Pens:/Bubbles:/Milk Cartons:/Water Pumps*. Boston, Mass.: Little, Brown and Co., 1979.

These four books do not fall into any traditional category of activity books, but they capture the essence of what science for young children ought to be. Each topic is only the starting point for exploring concepts through manipulation, construction, and interaction so that children may understand and appreciate the wonder of science. Most valuable resources to teachers and parents who understand the importance of young children's learning. The most celebrated of the four books is *Bubbles*, a valuable addition to the water tables in early childhood learning environments.

Chapter 3

SCIENCE BOOKS FOR CHILDREN

by Phylis Morrison

Introduction

Science books for children represent a real opportunity in the classroom. It is through such books
that a matter the teacher knows well, the teaching
and practice of reading, can be joined with another
matter, the human exploration and understanding of the
natural world. What often results is a learning experience for both teacher and child. The books available are extraordinary: over the last couple of decades
science books accessible to young children have increased in number and--more importantly--in quality.
They cover a broad range of subjects connected to
science and technology: books on cats and rats, on
bridges and spider's webs, on falling down and flying
up, on water and music and people, and, yes, on cab-
bages and kings too! Many of these books are so good
that they are often the best place for anyone, child
or adult, to get a first look at a subject new to him.
Here are books where children of various reading
skills can pursue some subject matter and learn new
information to bring to the group: all can become
teachers, teaching each other what they have learned.
Think of the discussions that can result among children
who have read books with differing views on a subject.

But these books can also extend the range of reading materials, and of reading skills that children bring to them, in a way different from most other reading matter in schools. One page in a science book might contain food for much thought; perhaps the whole book need not be read. Nor does a science book necessarily require that the reader begin at the beginning: many different strategies work and are useful. Here reading becomes a tool for personal use, and not just an activity for the practice of skills.

Young children, especially young children who often watch television, have trouble grasping the subtle line in books between the imaginary and that of reality. Many children's science books offer a child real help in dealing with this important matter, building a bridge between experiments suggested by a book, but performed on the stuff of the real world. Of course, that opening up of experimental science to a child for his very own exploration, for his own growth fostered by his choice and energy, is one of the important reasons we want children to have the study of science in their lives.

Notice that I speak of science books for children, and not "children's science books," for there is a great difference between the two categories. Children's science books are to be found on the science shelves in the children's section of a library. An ordinary example of the genre is a book that has been written especially for children, often with a limited vocabulary, by an expert in the learning of reading-- or at least it has been edited by such an expert. Looking over a random score of those books, one comes to the conclusion that their central purpose is to entice children into doing more *reading*, and that that reading is conceived of as the act of sitting down with the book, opening it, starting to read at the beginning, going on to the end, and then being able to tell someone what the book said. Books of this style are slightly suspect as *science* books: while most are fine, some are really not enlarging the child's view of the natural world as a place full of opportunities for questions, observations, involvements and understandings, nor are they enlarging a

child's view of what a book can contain. Even while
admitting that the ordinary children's science book
is a rather nice book, something more interesting and
exciting is available, and can easily be put at the
service of children.

One way to become aware of this broader view of
children's science books is to notice what categories
they might fall into. For instance, one category that
is always well represented in this field are books
that explore something about a single species of animal. *The Gull's Way* is a wonderful example of such a
book: a field biologist tells in his own words what
he has seen of gulls' behavior one summer on an isolated island in Maine. Except for the somewhat unusual
circumstance that this book was written by a scientist,
the category is a familiar one. We would not want
children to have only this one kind of book, however.

How then does the list of categories become en-
larged? After one has listed the kinds of books on
the school library's science shelves--life science,
the study of the earth, the chemical and physical sciences and so on, the biographies of scientists--there
is still much more. For example, there are adult
books that are easy for children to use: many coffee
table and reference books, as well as fieldguides,
fall easily into this category. And if one views
science more broadly, then many books whose primary
category is something else--art or history or story
telling--can also prove fruitful. After all, the
fairy tales that were collected in the last century
by the brothers Grimm are now seen to be a part of
the stream of anthropology, and we may add all such
works to our list of science books for children. Looking in another direction, many games and puzzles are
really applied mathematics and can provide a broader
way to look at that subject, and one that is a lot of
fun. Another category might concern itself with books
that teach the scientists' skills of observation.
While a book like Geraldine Flanagan's *Window into an
Egg* is an obvious example, so is Remy Charlip's *Thirteen*
or any of the books of Tana Hoban. But what about
Margaret Wise Brown's *Goodnight Moon*? Perhaps it be-
longs on that list as well, and in putting it there

we will have learned something new about the processes
of science.

The list of books that follows could be an entire-
ly different list. Excellent books abound and any of
the titles could be easily replaced by others just as
good. What is special about this list is its range:
it represents many kinds of books that are useful to
children coming to know about science. It is also a
rough guide to what it takes, at the ten-year-old
level, to be an informed layman.

The list is strongly skewed and is in no way indicative of the relative numbers of books published
each year in the various categories. The published
books lean quite heavily to subjects with a strong
emotional effect--subjects related to nature and especially animals are most heavily represented in the
publishers' annual lists. That this should be so for
young children seems a pity, for while all of us have
to depend to some extent upon the work of experts in
fields such as animal behavior--think of the work of
Jane Goodall with the chimpanzees--observing the behavior of the moon in the sky or of our own shadows
are experiences all of us can have at first hand. We
can all be happy that the quality of books that can
lead children into this world of personal experience
tends to be so very high, making up in quality for
their smaller relative numbers.

BIBLIOGRAPHY

Adkins, Jan. *Heavy Equipment*. New York: Charles
    Scribner's Sons, 1980.
        Categories: fieldguide
        Grade range: 1 to 4

    Good drawings of construction machinery at work,
    showing the telltale details.

————. *Moving Heavy Things*. Boston, Mass.: Houghton Mifflin Company, 1980.
  Categories: technical, observation, exploration
  Grade range: 3 to 8

Very real loads are shown, as well as the simplest ways of using human strength to move them. Children especially should be impressed by what large loads can be moved by small people.

Aliki. *Corn Is Maize*. New York: Thomas Y. Crowell, 1976.
  Categories: biology, anthropology, single species
  Grade range: 1 to 3

This talented and thoughtful children's author here provides a look at both the anthropology and the economic botany of this great American crop.

————. *My Five Senses*. New York: Thomas Y. Crowell, 1962.
  Categories: perception
  Grade range: 1 to 3

A first look at the individual qualities of the inborn instruments of science.

Ancona, George. *Team Work*. New York: Thomas Y. Crowell Company, 1983.
  Categories: anthropology
  Grade range: 2 to 5

A wonderful photographic evocation of real work, especially the cooperative sort of work that brings different skills together on a task.

Anno, Mitsumato. *Anno's Counting House*. New York: Philomel Books, 1977.
  Categories: mathematics, observation
  Grade range: K to 3

The magical master of ten thousand truly-seen details shows us what happens when ten people move
from one crowded house into an empty one. There is
much to count, and counting to think about.

————. *Anno's U.S.A.* New York: Philomel Books,
1983.
   Categories: anthropology
   Grade range: 1 onward

A journey across our land and across its years,
crowded with events familiar--is that Tom Sawyer?--
and new. Not a word, but much reading nonetheless.

Bager, Bartel. *Nature as Designer, a Botanical Art
Study.* New York: Reinhold Publishing Corp., 1966.
   Categories: biology, observation, structures
   Grade range: 3 onward

Plant parts, and especially seeds and their holding vessels, are explored for their great beauty.

Barnaby, Ralph. *How to Make and Fly Paper Airplanes.*
New York: Bantam Books, 1968.
   Categories: technology, exploration
   Grade range: 4 onward

An easy to manage in-school activity.

Baskin, Leonard. *Hosie's Alphabet.* New York: Viking
Press, 1972.
   Categories: observation, biology
   Grade range: Kindergarten onward

A loving master has painted wonders displayed in
twenty-six ways.

Baylor, Byrd. *Before You Came This Way.* New York:
E.P. Dutton & Co., 1969.
   Categories: anthropology
   Grade range: Kindergarten onward

An evocative calling forth of our southwestern
past, for the very young, that includes a strong
sense of time and respect for our forbears.

Benton, Michael. *The Dinosaur Encyclopedia*. New
  York: Wanderer Books, 1984.
    Categories: fieldguide, paleontology
    Grade range: 3 onward

Mainly a fieldguide, with clear information relating to size, and very accessible.

Beskow, Elsa. *Pelle's New Suit*. New York: Harper &
  Row, Publishers, 1929.
    Categories: technology, anthropology, story, classic
    Grade range: Kindergarten to 3

Pelle understands how a suit is made. He has a
grandmother who spins and one who weaves. He him-
self knows enough about dyeing.

Boeke, Kees. *Cosmic View, the Universe in 40 Jumps*.
  New York: John Day Company, Inc., 1973.
    Categories: scaling, astronomy, unification of
      science, classic
    Grade range: 4 onward

A great classic that tells you where you are and
also where--and how big--everything else is.

Bradkin, Cheryl G. *The Seminole Patchwork Book*.
  Atlanta, Ga,: Yours Truly, 1980.
    Categories: anthropology, mathematics
    Grade range: 4 onward

One of many excellent guides to the mathematical
activity of patchwork quilting.

Brady, Irene. *Wild Mouse*. New York: Charles Scribner's
  Sons, 1976.

Categories: biology, observation, single species
Grade range: Kindergarten to 6

How to watch a wild mouse, and the rewards. This
tiny book shows how profound the most ordinary subject matter of science can be for the very young.
The artist/author both draws the small events and
keeps a simple observational journal--something
children could do also.

Brown, Margaret Wise. *Goodnight Moon*. New York:
Scholastic Books, 1984.
    Categories: perception, observation, story
    Grade range: Pre-school to 3

A tiny classic of mood and observation, very rich
in its exploration of household sounds. Written to
be a story, but containing more than that. Any of
the books by this talented and caring author will
enrich a classroom.

Brown, Vinson. *Knowing the Outdoors in the Dark*.
New York: Collier Books, 1973.
    Categories: fieldguide, ecology, observation,
       perception
    Grade range: 4 onward

A fieldguide to the night and to beasts and scents
and sounds. No doubt the things that go "bump" are
there as well. We are told how to recognize all
this without needing sight.

Brown, Wyatt. *Kites*. New York: Golden Press.
    Categories: technology, materials
    Grade range: 3 onward

An introduction to a joyful activity that encourages both the skillful use of materials and an
exploration of the properties of air.

Burton, Virginia. *Life Story*. Boston, Mass.: Hough-
ton Mifflin Company, 1977.
   Categories: geology, unification of science,
      classic
   Grade range: 2 to 6

   Evolution seen at a single location on Cape Ann,
Massachusetts. The subject matter is grand: the
whole evolution of our earth, the great sphere and
all that lives on it, and all that is made by the
creatures that live here. A classic.

Charlip, Remy. *Thirteen*. New York: Parents' Magazine
Press, 1975.
   Categories: observation, counting, beauty
   Grade range: 1 onward

   No words, but thirteen concurrent stories, full
of exquisite detail, both hilarious and profound,
to puzzle out and wonder at.

Cobb, Vicki. *How to Really Fool Yourself*. New York:
J.B. Lippincott Company, 1981.
   Categories: perception, experiment
   Grade range: 4 to 7

   About sensory illusions, with many things to try.

Collier Books. *Photo Atlas of the United States*.
New York: Collier Books.
   Categories: maps, geology
   Grade range: 5 onward

   A satellite photo atlas in which the unity of the
map and the satellite photograph can be understood.

Cosgrove, Margaret. *Bone for Bone*. New York: Dodd,
Mead, 1968.
   Categories: biology, paleontology
   Grade range: 3 to 6

Comparative anatomy, with much that's easy to
learn, because we share some of the same bone structures.

Darling, Louis. *The Gull's Way*. New York: William
Morrow and Co., Inc., 1965.
Categories: biology, observation, ecology, classic,
single species
Grade range: 3 to 8

This life of the herring gulls on a rocky island
in New England is careful behavioral research, but
it is told in a poetic way. The author's field photographs provide highly convincing evidence for what
we are told about.

De Regniers, Beatrice. *The Shadow Book*. San Diego,
Calif.: Harcourt Brace Jovanovich, 1960.
Categories: physics, geometry
Grade range: Kindergarten to 3

This is a book about the way shadows work in
which the carefully chosen photographs tell more
than the words do.

Dietrich, R.V. *Stones*. New York: W.H. Freeman Co.,
1980.
Categories: geology, observation
Grade range: 5 onward

A serious geology of stones and pebbles, and much
lore to go with it. Here is a way to start understanding mineralogy with a modest kit.

Dietz, Betty, and Olatunji Dietz. *Musical Instruments
of Africa*. New York: John Day Company, 1965.
Categories: anthropology, physics
Grade range: 3 to 8

A look at some different ways of making sounds.

Dockstader, Frederick. *Indian Art in America*. Green-
wich, Conn.: New York Graphic Society, 1973.
Categories: anthropology, materials, beauty
Grade range: 4 onward

A fine book that shares the wonderful artifacts
of earlier Americans.

Ennion, E.A., and N. Tinbergen. *Tracks*. New York:
Oxford University Press, 1967.
Categories: biology, ecology, observation, classic
Grade range: 1 onward

Only people whose own work it is to watch the beach
so carefully could give us this spare, clear view of
what they see.

Flanagan, Geraldine. *Window into an Egg*. New York:
Young Scott Books, 1969.
Categories: biology, observation
Grade range: 3 to 6

In a series of wonderfully clear photographs we
are shown the development of a chick within its egg.
The luckiest children will have the real event hap-
pening in their classroom as well.

Freedman, Russel. *Hanging On: How Animals Carry Their
Young*. New York: Holiday House, Inc., 1977.
Categories: biology
Grade range: Kindergarten to 4

These photographs will enlarge children's knowledge and understanding of this subject and provide
plenty of laughter.

Fuchs, Erich. *Looking at Maps*. New York: Abelard-
Schuman Ltd., 1976.
Categories: geology, maps
Grade range: 2 to 5

Help in thinking through and understanding this
important subject.

Gallob, Edward. *City Leaves, City Trees*. New York:
Charles Scribner's Sons, 1972.
    Categories: biology, ecology, physical science
    Grade range: 2 to 8

Large photograms, with a discussion of the trees
and of how the images were made.

Gans, Roma. *Birds at Night*. New York: Thomas Y.
Crowell Company, 1976.
    Categories: biology, ecology
    Grade range: Kindergarten to 2

————. *Birds Eat and Eat and Eat*. New York: Thomas
Y. Crowell Company, 1975.
    Categories: biology, ecology
    Grade range: Kindergarten to 2

————. *It's Nesting Time*. New York: Thomas Y. Crowell
Company, 1977.
    Categories: biology, ecology
    Grade range: Kindergarten to 2

This talented author provides scientific information on birds through storytelling and effective
illustrations. It is adapted to children's cognitive
and interest levels.

Gardner, Martin. *Codes, Ciphers and Secret Writing*.
New York: Dover Press, 1984.
    Categories: mathematics, language
    Grade range: 4 onward

Another way of looking at the raw material of reading and an enlargement of understanding that is useful to many children. The underlying patterns and
order of language are nicely explored.

Garelick, May. *What's Inside?* New York: Young Scott
  Books, 1955; Scholastic Book Services, 1968.
    Categories: biology, observation
    Grade range: 1 to 5

  A picture book that leads to thought and to good
  discussion.

Gerster, Georg. *Grand Design.* New York: Paddington
  Press, Ltd., 1976.
    Categories: geology, beauty
    Grade range: 1 onward

  A really beautiful book of photographs, intended
  for an adult audience, showing many things about the
  world, both familiar and strange, from several hundred feet up. A few books of this caliber should be
  a part of every child's experience.

Girl Scouts and Boy Scouts of America. *Merit Badge
  Books.* New York: Girl Scouts of America; Irving,
  Tex.: Boy Scouts of America.
    Categories: everything, technical, biology,
      physics, experiments, observation

  A treasure house of information designed for self-
  instruction on subjects from surveying to bookbinding.
  Not just for scouts.

Gjersvik, Maryanne. *Green Fun.* Old Greenwich, Conn.:
  The Chatham Press, Inc., 1975.
    Categories: technical, biology, experiments
    Grade range: Kindergarten onward

  Games and recreations invented long ago that use
  the materials of the natural world. For the young
  and young at heart.

Golden Press. *The Golden Nature Guides.* New York:
  Golden Press, 1973.

Categories: reference, fieldguides
Grade range: 2 onward

Trees, sea shells, insects, stars, etc. Cheap,
small, accessible, and wonderful. You need to have
these around.

Goor, Ron, and Nancy Goor. *Shadows, Here, There and
Everywhere*. New York: Thomas Y. Crowell Company,
1981.
Categories; physics
Grade range: Kindergarten to 3

This is a wonderful subject that uses familiar experience to enlarge one's grasp of the physical
world.

Grunfeld, Frederic. *Games of the World*. New York:
Ballantine Books, 1975.
Categories: mathematics, anthropology, experiments,
beauty
Grade range: 2 onward

Fine photographs of the original settings of many
games, with instructions on how to play them and how
to make the necessary equipment. Anthropology for
beginners.

Guilcher, J.M., and R.H. Noailles. *A Tree Is Born*.
New York: Sterling Publishing Co., 1964.
Categories: biology, observation
Grade range: 4 onward

Acorn to acorn, chestnut to chestnut, pine cone
to pine cone; we are shown the cycles, revealing
how the seed splits, the leaf unfolds, the bud
bursts. A very modest book, but one that was a
large and careful labor to make.

Halstead, L.B., and B. Halstead. *Dinosaurs*. New York:
Blandford Press, 1981.

Categories: paleontology, fieldguide
Grade range: 3 onward

Most of what I, a schoolteacher, know of dinosaurs
was taught to me by wonderfully knowledgeable third
graders who drew them, sculpted them, and knew all
of their names. Perhaps this book is where they
came by their expertise?

Hamerstrom, Frances. *Adventure of the Stone Man*.
Trumansburg, N.Y.: The Crossing Press, 1977.
Categories: anthropology, story
Grade range: 3 to 6

A fictionalized tale of high archaeology, very
exciting and with fine characterizations. The artifacts the tale is about are Magdallenian, and the
book presents a very convincing view of French
domestic life in the last century.

Hammond, Inc. *The Hammond Almanac of a Million Facts*.
Maplewood, N.J.: Hammond, Inc.
Categories: reference
Grade range: 4 onward.

Every classroom needs such a book to follow up on
serendipitous ideas. Along the way the children will
learn about uncovering facts, and about reaching out
for what they don't know.

Hay, John. *The Sandy Shore*. Old Greenwich, Conn.:
The Chatham Press, Inc., 1968.
Categories: fieldguide, ecology, observation
Grade range: 1 onward

An informal fieldguide to an unusual part of the
earth with wonderfully enticing sketches.

Hoban, Tana. *Big Ones, Little Ones*. New York:
William Morrow and Co., Inc., Greenwillow Books,
1976.

Categories: Observation, geometry
Grade range: Kindergarten to 3

A fine photographer shares a fresh way of seeing things in terms of their size in this imaginative photo-essay.

————. *Look Again*. New York: Macmillan Publishing Co., 1971.
  Categories: observation
  Grade range: Kindergarten to 3

Abstract and concrete images by a writer who knows how to make her photographs convey true subject matter, and who manages to do this with humor.

————. *More Than One*. New York: William Morrow and Co., 1981.
  Categories: mathematics, counting
  Grade range: Kindergarten to 2

For counting, and for thinking about counting. It's not as easy as you think!

Hofsinde, Robert. *Indian Music Makers*. New York: William Morrow and Co., Inc., 1967.
  Categories: physics, anthropology
  Grade range: 2 to 5

American musical instruments and very easy suggestions for fabrication.

Holling, Holling Clancy. *Paddle-to-the Sea*. Boston, Mass.: Houghton Mifflin Company, 1941.
  Categories: geography, ecology, maps, story, technology, classic
  Grade range: 3 to 6

A fine tale of a sojourner through the American North, but with many extra drawings to show how things worked: carving, trading, sawmills, water-locks, and tools of many kinds.

Jacobs, Francine. *Supersaurus*. New York: J.P. Putnam's Sons, 1982.
    Categories: paleontology, biology, single species
    Grade range: 1 to 3

Even a small book for the very young can be about
a subject at the forefront of its science. This one
is about the new work being done on "warm-blooded"
dinosaurs.

Jenness, Aylette, and L. Kroeber. *A Life of Their Own*.
New York: Thomas Y. Crowell Company, 1975.
    Categories: anthropology, technology
    Grade range: 4 to 7

A look at the lives of a peasant family in Guate-
mala. We learn of the many skills--both familiar
and unfamiliar--that are needed in this way of life.

Johnson, Pauline. *Creating with Paper*. Seattle, Wash.:
University of Washington Press, 1975.
    Categories: materials, experiment, structures,
      beauty
    Grade range: 3 onward

Papers as a structural material and the exploration of surface. A beautiful old book, and an end-
less resource.

Jones, Madeline. *The Mysterious Flexagons*. New York:
Crown Publishers, Inc., 1966.
    Categories: mathematics, geometry, experiments
    Grade range: 4 to 8

These ingenious paperfolds exemplify the mathematics of combinatorics.

Kevles, Bettyann. *Watching the Wild Apes*. New York:
E.P. Dutton & Co., 1976.
    Categories: biology, ecology
    Grade range: 4 to 9

A good narrative on the field work of three women who studied primates.

Kitamura, Satoshi. *What's Inside: The Alphabet Book*. New York: Farrar, Straus & Giroux, Inc., 1985.
   Categories: observation
   Grade range: Kindergarten to 4

This book DEMANDS all of the observational skills of the reader, and rewards him/her with much delight.

Kornerup, A., and J.H. Wanschler. *Methuen Handbook of Colour*. New York: Barnes and Noble, Inc., 1984.
   Categories: physics, technology, fieldguide
   Grade range: 3 onward

A fieldguide to color with many examples and tools for further exploration. Color language is not left out. Pervasive as it may be, color is a difficult subject and the broadening of experience that this book fosters is a useful step for anyone.

Kraske, Robert. *The Twelve Million Dollar Note*. New York: Thomas Nelson, Inc., 1977.
   Categories: geology, exploration
   Grade range: 4 onward

Stories about messages put in bottles and about ocean currents. A wonderful further step for classes who have read Paddle-to-the-Sea.

Kuskin, Karla. *A Space Story*. New York: Harper & Row, Publishers, 1978.
   Categories: astronomy, story
   Grade range: 2 to 4

A story about stars and planets, including ours and, perhaps, theirs....

Larsson, Carl. *A Farm*. New York: J.P. Putnam's Sons, 1976.
    Categories: observation, anthropology
    Grade range: 1 onward

    A famous Swedish painter recorded with great affection the old farm where his family lived.

Lasky, Kathryn. *The Weaver's Gift*. New York: Frederick Warne & Co., Inc., 1981.
    Categories: anthropology, story
    Grade range: Kindergarten to 3

    How a blanket came to be made: the place, the sheep, the shearing, the spinning, the weaving, and the person for whom it was made.

Lionni, Leo. *A Fish Is a Fish*. New York: Pantheon Books, 1970.
    Categories: biology
    Grade range: Kindergarten to 3

    This well-known author of children's books tells the story of a fish that got intrigued by the tales of his friend, the frog, and tried to visit land. Excellent illustrations.

Litwin, Wallace. *Ostrich*. New York: Coward-McCann & Geohegan, Inc., 1973.
    Categories: single species, biology
    Grade range: 1 to 4

Macaulay, David. *Castle*. Boston, Mass.: Houghton Mifflin Company, 1977.
    Categories: structures, technology, anthropology
    Grade range: 1 onward

    Wonderful detailed drawings of a castle and all its parts.

MacFarlane, Iris. *The Mouth of the Night*. New York:
   William Morrow and Co., Inc., Macmillan Books, 1973.
      Categories: anthropology, folktales
      Grade range: 3 onward

   Vivid Irish folktales.

MacGregor, Anne, and Scott MacGregor. *Bridges, A
   Project Book*. New York: Lothrop, Lee & Shepard Co.,
   1981.
      Categories: technology, exploration, materials,
         structures
      Grade range: 3 to 8

   Thoughtful suggestions for building, using simple
   materials.

McNulty, Faith. *How to Dig a Hole to the Other Side
   of the World*. New York: Harper & Row, Publishers,
   1979.
      Categories: geology, story
      Grade range: Kindergarten to 4

   Actually what its title suggests, but both hilarious and thought provoking.

Milne, Lorus, and M. Milne. *Nature's Clean-Up Crew*.
   New York: Dodd, Mead, 1982.
      Categories: biology, ecology, single species
      Grade range: 3 to 7

   The sense of authenticity that is felt by a reader
   when authors tell about their own work is exemplified
   in this book. The unusual behavior of the burying
   beetles would not be easily believable if the precise detail was not presented so vividly.

Munari, Bruno. *From Afar It Is an Island*. New York:
   The World Publishing Company, 1972.
      Categories: geology, observation
      Grade range: Kindergarten to 4

Another human use of geology, a rich one, seen with perceptive artist's eyes.

Newton, James. *Rain Shadow.* New York: Thomas Y. Crowell Company, 1983.
Categories: geology
Grade range: 2 to 5

Drawings and text that reveal a way to look at the relationship between landscape and weather.

Nicholson, B.E., S.G. Harrison, G.B. Masefield, and M. Wallis. *The Oxford Book of Food Plants.* New York: Oxford University Press, 1969.
Categories: biology, fieldguide, beauty
Grade range: 1 onward

Color paintings and short clear articles about our fruits and vegetables, the ones you see at the supermarket here and also far away. It's great to have a field guide to something that is really part of every person's life.

Northshore Rock Club. *Collecting Sites In and Around New England.*
Categories: geology, local
Grade range: 5 onward

Very local, mimeographed pamphlet. It is important to gather such material on one's own locality and one of the ways to do this is to consult a professor of geology at the State University.

Ottewell, Guy. *To Know the Stars.* Greenville, S.C.: Furman University, 1984.
Categories: astronomy, fieldguide
Grade range: 4 to 8

This explores the night sky for a year, helping us to come to know our way around it across the seasons. Full of Ottewell's hand drawn sky maps.

————. *View from the Earth*. Greenville, S.C.:
   Furman University, 1982.
   Categories: astronomy, fieldguide
   Grade range: 3 to 12

   This is Ottewell's astronomical guide for young
or less experienced people. Here you can learn to
find your way around the sky.

Pallas, Norvin. *Code Games*. New York: Sterling Pub-
   lishing Co., 1983.
   Categories: mathematics, exploration, language
   Grade range: 4 to 8

   Another way to study language and the sense of
order that makes reading possible.

Parker, Nancy. *The President's Car*. New York: Thomas
   Y. Crowell Company, 1981.
   Categories: technology
   Grade range: 3 to 7

   If you think about it, you will realize that the
cars of former Presidents form a history of modern
transportation. Funny, too!

Paull, John, and Dorothy Paull. *Nature Takes Shape*.
   Harmondsworth: Ladybird Books, Penguin, 1980.
   Categories: biology, mathematics
   Grade range: 3 to 6

   Here is an example of a very large series, the
Ladybird Books, from England. Small and very inexpensive, there is a book on almost any subject
imaginable.

Pelham, David. *Kites to Make and Fly*. New York: Pen-
   guin Books, 1982.
   Categories: technology, materials
   Grade range: 4 onward

Recipes for kites that will really fly and that are a manageable challenge to make. The opportunities for science learning in kite making and flying are great: everything from the technology of the materials used to questions of wind and weather is involved.

Pitseolak, P. *Pictures Out of My Life*. Seattle, Wash.: University of Washington Press, 1979.
Categories: anthropology, observation, beauty
Grade range: 4 onward

"My name is Pitseolak, the Eskimo word for the sea pigeon. When I see the Pitseolaks over the sea, I say, 'There go those lovely birds--that's me, flying!' I have lost the time when I was born...." Pitseolak is an Eskimo and an artist and this is her story. The book is beautifully illustrated with reproductions of her works, many of them in color.

Prance, Ghilean, and K.B. Sandved. *Leaves*. New York: Crown Publishers, Inc., 1985.
Categories: biology, observation, beauty
Grade range: 3 onward

A beautiful photographic essay on the many properties of leaves.

Rahn, Joan. *Grocery Store Zoology*. New York: Atheneum Publishers, 1977.
Categories: biology, exploration
Grade range: 4 to 8

Again, the fresh exploration of the familiar.

Rand McNally. *The International Atlas*. Skokie, Ill.: Rand McNally, Inc.
Categories: maps, geography, reference, beauty
Grade range: 3 onward

All classrooms should contain an atlas to be con-
sulted often about our world and its events, and a
dictionary to be used as a fieldguide to our language. We particularly like this atlas because it
shows subtle relief, allowing one to come to know
the physical world in relation to the political one,
but any atlas from $5 to $100 would be well used in
a classroom.

Reich, Hans. *The World from Above*. New York: Hill &
Wang, 1968.
  Categories: geology, observation
  Grade range: 3 onward

A book of beautiful aerial photos of countryside
and town, to give us an overview of ourselves at a
scale all of us can understand and learn from.

Reid, George, and H. Zim. *Pond Life*. New York: Golden
Press, 1967.
  Categories: fieldguide, observation
  Grade range: 3 onward

This modest little book could spark a whole year
of work for a class with a nearby pond.

Rey, H.A. *The Stars, a New Way to See Them*. Boston,
Mass.: Houghton Mifflin Company, 1967.
  Categories: astronomy, fieldguide, classic
  Grade range: 3 to 7

A sky atlas with maps, constellations, and seasons.

Rhodes, D. *How to Read a City Map*. Los Angeles,
Calif.: Elk Grove Press, Inc., 1970.
  Categories: maps
  Grade range: 2 to 5

Features both photographs and the maps made from
them.

Rice, Stanley. *Getting Started in Prints and Patterns*. New York: Bruce Publishing, 1971.
   Categories: geometry, technology
   Grade range: 2 to 7

What is presented here could be seen either as an art activity or as a way to explore the geometrical possibilities of surface.

Rukeyser, Muriel. *Bubbles*. San Diego, Calif.: Harcourt Brace Jovanovich, 1967.
   Categories: observation, poetry
   Grade range: 2 to 5

What a real poet saw.

Salvadori, Mario. *Building: From Caves to Skyscrapers*. New York: Atheneum Publishers, 1985.
   Categories: structures, materials
   Grade range: 3 to 9

A book about structures written for children by a man who for years taught the subject to graduate students before he taught it to children.

Scharf, David. *Magnifications*. New York: Schocken Books, Inc., 1978.
   Categories, biology, observation
   Grade range: 3 onward

An eye-opener into the world of the very small and what can be found there.

Selsam, Millicent. *Popcorn*. New York: William Morrow and Co., Inc., 1976.
   Categories: single species, biology
   Grade range: Kindergarten to 3

This fine writer shows the plant, the growing, the seed, and the surprising result.

————. *The Plants We Eat*. New York: William Morrow
and Co., Inc., 1981.
  Categories: biology, anthropology
  Grade range: Kindergarten to 6

The familiar things we eat are shown to us in
another aspect, giving us a richer picture of the
familiar.

Selsam, Millicent, and J. Hunt. *A First Look at Leaves*.
New York: Walker and Company, 1972.
  Categories: biology
  Grade range: Kindergarten to 3

For beginning to notice differences.

Spier, Peter. *Gobble Growl Grunt*. New York: Doubleday
and Company, Inc., 1979.
  Categories: observation, phonics, biology
  Grade range: 1 to 4

It may be a phonic lesson, but it is truly what
the beasts say, because Peter Spier listened. Read
it aloud, a whole class at a time!

Stecher, Miriam, and A.S. Kandell. *Max, the Music
Maker*. New York: Lothrop, Lee & Shepard Co., 1980.
  Categories: physics
  Grade range: Kindergarten to 2

Max, who may be five, knows a lot about sounds and
how they are made. The photographs in this brief
book let us share that vividly.

Stone, Harris. *Chemistry of a Lemon*. Englewood
Cliffs, N.J.: Prentice-Hall, Inc., 1966.
  Categories: physical science, chemistry
  Grade range: 3 to 7

A dozen varied experiments, all using lemons.

Svensson, Sam. *Handbook of Seaman's Ropework*. New
   York: Dodd, Mead, 1972.
      Categories: materials, geometry
      Grade range: 4 onward

   The ways to tie knots, and what they are for.

Symonds, G.W. *The Tree Identification Book*. New York:
   M. Barrows and Company, 1973.
      Categories: biology, fieldguide, observation
      Grade range: 3 onward

   This is the easiest of the fieldguides for children
   to use because of its unique organizational scheme.

Van Soelen, Philip. *Cricket in the Grass and Other
   Stories*. San Francisco, Calif.: Sierra Club Books,
   1979.
      Categories: ecology, observation
      Grade range: 1 to 4
      Mostly pictures, but pictures that can be read to
   find a tale of the web of relationships we call
   ecology.

Wahl, John. *I Can Count the Petals of a Flower*. 2nd
   ed. Reston, Va.: NCTM, 1985.
      Categories: counting, observation
      Grade range: Kindergarten to 3

   We are shown flowers with one, with two, with
   many petals, and also some surprises.

Walter, Marion. *Make a Bigger Puddle, Make a Smaller
   Worm*. New York: M. Evans and Company, Inc., 1972.
      Categories: mathematics, geometry
      Grade range: 1 to 4

   Symmetry mathematics and a mirror to explore it
   with.

The Way Things Work. New York: Simon & Schuster,
    Inc., 1967.
        Categories: technology, physics
        Grade range: 4 onward

    A page of text and a drawing or two explaining
each of a couple of hundred gadgets, from a jet
plane to a fluorescent lamp. Here is a "reference"
book that is really an invitation for study, especially a page at a time. A version for young
readers has also been published.

Wentz, Bud. *Paper Movie Machines*. San Francisco,
    Calif.: Troubador Press, 1975.
        Categories: technology, perception, exploration
        Grade range: 4 onward

    A book of splendidly satisfying re-creations of
old-fashioned movie machines, along with an explanation of how they work.

Wilkins, Marne. *The Long Ago Lake, a Child's Book of
    Nature Lore & Crafts*. New York: Sierra Club, Charles
    Scribner's Sons, 1978.
        Categories: biology, ecology, exploration
        Grade range: 3 to 8

    A way to use materials and to learn how they have
been used by others.

Wolkstein, Diane. *8,000 Stones, A Chinese Folktale*.
    New York: Doubleday and Company, Inc., 1972.
        Categories: physics, anthropology, story
        Grade range: 2 to 5

    A retelling of an old Chinese folktale, with a
science story folded within it.

Wyler, Rose, and G. Ames. *Secrets in Stones*. New
    York: Four Winds, 1972.
        Categories: geology, observation
        Grade range: 1 to 4

A treasure of a geology book for any beginner. Mostly about pebbles.

Zaslavski, Claudia. *Tic Tac Toe and Other Three-in-a-Row Games.* New York: Thomas Y. Crowell Company, 1982.
   Categories: mathematics, exploration
   Grade range: 3 to 7

   Games and the people who play them.

Zim, Herbert, and P.R. Shaffer. *Rocks and Minerals.* New York: Simon and Schuster Inc., 1957.
   Categories: geology, fieldguide
   Grade range: 2 onward

   One of the classic fieldguides organized by this author/editor.

Periodicals

National Geographic World. National Geographic, Washington, D.C.
   Categories: periodical, anthropology, biology
   Grade range: 3 to 6

   One of the excellent magazines for classroom use, this one with genuine help for the teacher included.

Ranger Rick's Nature Magazine. National Wildlife Federation, Washington, D.C.
   Catgeories: periodical, biology, ecology
   Grade range: Kindergarten to 3

   Every classroom should have a magazine or two with its surprises every month. The material in this one is well put together and the illustrations are as good as in the very best adult magazines.

Sky Calendar. Abrams Planetarium, Lansing, Mich.
   Categories: astronomy, observation, periodical
   Grade range: 3 onward

   A one-page-per-month periodical that brings the
news of the simple heavenly events: where the moon
will be at sunset, what the bright planet near the
moon tonight is. A treasure.

The Curious Naturalist. Massachusetts Audubon Society.
   Categories: periodical, biology, ecology
   Grade range: 2 to 6

   Another of the fine classroom magazines.

Chapter 4

SCIENCE EDUCATION FOR THE SPECIAL CHILD

This essay examines current thinking on science
education for the special child and the key resources
that are available in that area. During the last
twenty-five years in particular there have been
challenges to involve special children in effective
learning. There have also been struggles and vic-
tories concerning the best way to accomplish this
goal. Legislation has been passed that entitles *all*
children to equal opportunity in education.

Literature supports the notion that learning
science is essential for children's growth and development, and especially for young children's sensory approaches in exploring the world around them.
During this action-based interactive process which is
science learning, children develop process skills in
observing, relating, sorting, classifying, comparing,
and predicting--all so necessary in understanding and
appreciating physical objects, natural phenomena, and
living things.

These assumptions, about how young children's
involvement with science contributes to their development gain a new dimension when we think of special
children. This is particularly so because the term
includes children with a wide range of handicaps--
physical, emotional, and intellectual. The children
therefore mandate a stronger emphasis in the planning
of their educational experiences so that they may be
provided with compensatory and therapeutic activities

that will enable them to live fuller lives in a world so compact with knowledge and problem solving possibilities.

Many science educators have addressed the issue of teaching science to special children; more specifically, the National Science Teachers' Association (NSTA) devoted an entire conference to the exploration and documentation of the role of science in the lives of physically handicapped children. During this 1978 NSTA conference in Washington, D.C., a wide range of information was presented that included evidence on the importance of teaching science to children with visual, auditory and orthopedic impairments. In conclusion the conferees agreed on the need for more science teaching in the learning environments of special children and recommended to teachers a wide range of sources on how and where to seek assistance in enriching their teaching of science. A bibliography and an exhaustive list of organizations that concern themselves with science and the handicapped are also included in their publication, *Sourcebook Science Education and the Physically Handicapped*. The book is a valuable companion to all professionals who focus their teaching on special children.

The compensatory approach in teaching science to special children is the theme of Haldary and Cohen in their monumental book, *Laboratory Science and Art for Blind, Deaf and Emotionally Disturbed Children*. The book is written for preservice and inservice teachers who plan to meet the needs of the handicapped child in or out of the classroom. The science activities that compensate for certain handicaps are adapted from well-known Elementary Science Curricula: ESS (Elementary Science Study), S-APA (Science-A Process Approach) and SCIS (Science Curriculum Improvement Study). The authors underscore the importance of understanding the handicap, the physical and emotional limitations of the child, and what adaptations are required to meet the child's needs so that he/she can enjoy effective learning.

Furthermore, a strong argument is presented in Haldary and Cohen for the ways in which art and science "share common learning experiences and procedures"

and how discoveries in science can be reinforced
through art projects. This interplay between the
two disciplines facilitates further children's understanding of the nature of the physical world and its
natural phenomena. For example, in testing the
floating and sinking concept where children make
clay boats in a water table, a blind child has the
possibility to explore different shapes and how they
relate to sinking and floating. These tactile observations can be clarified through an art project in
wooden boat building and wood carving where the child
is creating the simple representational form of a
boat. Thus, the interrelatedness of science and art
can help the handicapped child expand upon his tactile
experience and thus further clarify the physical
properties of floating/sinking structures. This sci-
ence/art relationship can be exploited to equal ad-
vantage with emotionally disturbed children. What it
provides is both a structure for the understanding
of physical properties and natural phenomena and an
outlet for artistic expression. Furthermore, the
sense of control they will experience from this activity will enhance their confidence and self-esteem
and will contribute therapeutically to their development.

The emphasis on the adaptation of science activities to accommodate the needs of special children
finds strong support in Mary Rowe's writings. She
highlights the concept of time, as an important
variable in the teaching of science for special children: the mentally retarded need more time to explore
and integrate their findings, the emotionally disturbed need more time to control their responses,
deaf children are slower in picking out visual information through lip readings, and blind students have
"no lead time." According to Rowe, teaching science
to the handicapped is more important than it is for
children without handicaps. She claims that the
physical world is not as available to them as to the
other children. The experiences that lead to explorations, observations, classification, measurements,
and so forth must be created so that children with
handicaps will have an equal opportunity to learn
about the world around them.

The following books clearly show the importance that science has in the development of the child with special needs. Although there are different opinions in the field, the works discussed in this essay and those listed in the bibliography provide a foundation that can be used as a springboard to more complete knowledge of the role of science in the education of special children.

BIBLIOGRAPHY

Brearley, M., et al. *The Teaching of Young Children.* New York: Schocken Books, 1969.

Flavell, John H. *Developmental Psychology of Jean Piaget.* New York: Van Nostrand, 1963.

Haldary, D.F., and S.H. Cohen. *Laboratory Science and Art for Blind, Deaf and Emotionally Disturbed Children.* Baltimore, Md.: Baltimore University Park Press, 1978.

Hawkins, D. "Messing About in Science." *Science and Children.* 2: 5-9. February 1965.

Hein, G. "Children's Science Is Another Culture." *Technology Review.* 1968.

Hochman, V., and M. Greenwald. *Science Experiences in Early Childhood.* New York: Bank Street College of Education Publications, 1963.

Hoffman, H.H., and K.S. Ricker. *Sourcebook in Science Education and the Physically Handicapped.* Washington, D.C.: N.S.T.A., 1979.

Landsdown, B., P.E. Blackwood, and P.F. Brandwein. *Teaching Elementary Science Through Investigation*

and *Colloquium*. New York: Harcourt Brace Jovanovich, 1971.

McIntyre, M. *Early Childhood and Science*. Washington,
D.C.: N.S.T.A., 1984.

Piaget, J. *The Child and Reality*. New York: Grossman
Publishers, 1972.

Rowe, Mary Budd. "Help Is Desired to Those in Need."
Science and Children. 12: 23-25. March 1975.

————. *Teaching Science as Continuous Inquiry: A
Basic*. New York: McGraw-Hill Book Co., 1978.

SUBJECT INDEX
FOR CHAPTERS 1 AND 2

Although all books may mention any of the topics listed
below, the references are to books that engage in a
discussion of the particular topics.

SUBJECT INDEX
FOR CHAPTER 3